D0340056

2 —

*Praise for*
## MY SOUL LOOKS BACK IN WONDER

"Juan Williams and his team have created another important contribution to understanding our society, its dynamics and its dilemmas. Listening to the voices in this book—the voices of the well-known and the unknown—we experience their struggles and how often their deeds were small steps that they needed to take, not knowing the consequences. We see people reaching beyond themselves, standing for dignity, respect, fairness, justice. We tend to think that it is the great heroes and she-roes that turn history, but *My Soul Looks Back in Wonder* shows us the underlying commitments that made the big steps possible. Substantial social change does not come from the top down, but from the bottom up. Breaking the barriers of segregation did not come from presidential or Congressional initiative, but from the determination of thousands of demonstrators, like those in Selma, Alabama, that led to the Voting Rights Act—truly a watershed moment in our history.

"When you read the compelling stories in this book, stories of conscience and courage, you will cry, you will laugh, you will remember, you will be inspired for the struggles that continue today."

—REV. JESSE L. JACKSON

"By searching out the personal rather than the pious, Williams has fashioned an original document about the tragically brief moment in which American democracy struggled to realize itself."

—TOM WICKER

"Juan Williams asks questions and elicits answers that help every American understand the black experience in this country. We have him to thank for the clearer, truer picture of the civil rights struggle that emerges from each page of *My Soul Looks Back in Wonder.*"

—JUDY WOODRUFF

"This is the real American story, the story of those who dared, dreamed, and some of whom died to see that America lived up to its professed ideals. Read it and be stirred, as I was, by the courage and idealism of that courageous band who challenged and remade America. They remain the real American heroes."

—HAYNES JOHNSON

AN END
TO BIAS
NOW!

TOLEDO

# MY SOUL BACK IN

## *Voices of the Civil*

Foreword DAVID HALBERSTAM
Afterword MARIAN WRIGHT EDELMAN

# LOOKS WONDER

## *Rights Experience*

Juan Williams

STERLING

COVER: A woman drinks from a segregated water fountain in Birmingham, Alabama, in 1956.

BACK COVER: A Salvadoran-turned-Californian makes waves at a 2003 rally for immigrant rights in Washington, D.C.

PAGES II–III: An expectant crowd of more than 250,000 gathers to hear Martin Luther King, Jr., and others during the March on Washington in 1963.

PRECEDING PAGES: Bridging the racial divide, young civil rights workers break into song en route to Mississippi during Freedom Summer, 1964.

AARP books publishes a wide range of titles on health, personal finance, lifestyle, and other subjects to enrich the lives of 50+ Americans. For more information, go to www.aarp.org/books/

AARP, established in 1958, is a nonprofit organization with more than 35 million members age 50 and older. The views expressed herein do not necessarily represent the policies of AARP and should not be construed as endorsements.



**Library of Congress Cataloging-in-Publication Data Available**

10 9 8 7 6 5 4 3 2

Published by Sterling Publishing Co., Inc.
387 Park Avenue South, New York, N.Y. 10016



Distributed in Canada by Sterling Publishing
℅Canadian Manda Group, 165 Dufferin Street
Toronto, Ontario, Canada M6K 3H6

Distributed in Great Britain by Chrysalis Books Group PLC
The Chrysalis Building, Bramley Road, London W10 6SP, England

Distributed in Australia by Capricorn Link (Australia) Pty. Ltd.
P.O. Box 704, Windsor, NSW 2756, Australia


*Manufactured in the United States of America*

Sterling ISBN 1-4027-1415-7

*To my mother, Alma,*
*and all the unsung heroes*
*who sacrificed to make*
*strong families.*

## HOW I GOT OVER

*How I got over,*
*How I got over, my Lord*
*And my soul looked back and wondered*
*How I got over, my Lord*

*The tallest tree in Paradise*
*The Christians call it tree of life*
*And my soul looked back and wondered*
*How I got over, my Lord*

*Lord, I've been 'buked and I've been scorned*
*And I've been talked 'bout as sure as you're born*
*And my soul looked back and wondered*
*How I got over, my Lord*

*Oh, Jordan's river is so chilly and cold*
*It will chill your body but not your soul*
*And my soul looked back and wondered*
*How I got over, my Lord*

ALSO BY JUAN WILLIAMS

*Thurgood Marshall: American Revolutionary*

*Eyes on the Prize: America's Civil Rights Years, 1954-1965*

*This Far by Faith: Stories from the African American Religious Experience*

# CONTENTS

CONTENTS

# Acknowledgments

This book came to life as a symphony. It is the creation of a team of very talented people, including editors, correspondents, researchers, and designers. Of course, the book's heart is in the personal stories of the people who agreed to sit down and talk into tape recorders about critical moments in their lives—and in American history. I am grateful to each of you for your time and most of all for your wisdom, your knowledge, and your spirit.

*My Soul Looks Back in Wonder* is part of the Voices of Civil Rights project, a collaboration between AARP and the Leadership Conference on Civil Rights (LCCR) to build the world's largest archive of firsthand accounts of the Civil Rights Movement. I would like to thank AARP CEO Bill Novelli, AARP president Marie Smith, and Voices project originator Rick Bowers for championing this initiative. Special thanks also go to LCCR chairwoman Dorothy Height, LCCR executive director Wade Henderson, and their board for their inclusive vision of civil rights in America. Born in the civil rights struggles of the 1950s, the LCCR—which represents more than 180 organizations—fights for justice every day and reflects the 21st century civil rights agenda as women, gays and lesbians, Asian Americans, Native Americans, and disabled Americans—indeed, all of us—join together to advance the cause of equality. Thanks also go to James Billington of the Library of Congress, where the Voices archive will ultimately be housed.

Many people worked behind the scenes to give life to this book. My former *Washington Post* colleague Megan Rosenfeld served as the book's chief of correspondents, expertly directing the team of reporters who fanned out across the country to capture the stories collected here. She followed a trail blazed by another *Post* veteran, Leah Latimer, who recruited and briefed the correspondents before moving on to become the editor of the Voices of Civil Rights website. I am especially grateful to Leah for coming up with the book's inspirational title, drawn from the spiritual "How I Got Over" *(page ix)*.

Among the correspondents who performed the critical job of getting the right people to talk was Ponchitta Pierce, a contributing editor at *Parade* magazine and a regular contributor to *AARP The Magazine*. "It was an inspiration to capture the voices of those who challenged this nation to end racism," she says of her work on *My Soul*. "Their optimism and commitment obligate the rest of us to continue the fight for a color-blind America."

Correspondent Joe Nick Patoski, a former staff writer for *Texas*

*Monthly,* saw the book as an opportunity to show the influence of popular culture on social change. "In music or pop culture," he says, "the color lines were being broken long before the laws said you could. Black musicians paved the way for Martin Luther King, Jr."

Vern Smith, a former national reporter and Atlanta bureau chief for *Newsweek,* was reminded of his own political awakening as he conducted interviews throughout the South. "I can recall the precise moment when young civil rights workers arrived in my hometown of Natchez, Mississippi, to lead voter registration drives and raise people's consciousness," he says. "To a young black kid, it was affirming and hopeful to see these people challenging the status quo. I realized they were changing Natchez forever."

Jimmie Briggs says his work as a correspondent on the book led him to a better understanding of how "various American movements for racial, labor, Latino, and gay rights overlapped." A freelance writer and former reporter for *Emerge* magazine, Briggs began to see connections between the voices in this book and the events he covers around the world.

Correspondent Lester Sloan did a superb job of drawing out stories from his interview subjects. A former photographer for *Newsweek,* Sloan now also does freelance writing. His experience taking pictures around the world heightened his appreciation for ordinary people who surprise themselves by standing up to make history.

Other correspondents included Texas writer Dick J. Reavis, author of the civil rights memoir *If White Kids Die;* freelance writer and NPR commentator Bonny Wolf; and author Tom Miller, whose nine books include *The Panama Hat Trail, On the Border,* and *Trading with the Enemy.*

Hugh Delehanty, AARP Publications' editor in chief, was a brilliant and steady hand on this book. This is his baby—his joy. The book is a testament to the quality of his ideas as well as his ability to handle editorial pressure. Hugh got me to explore my perceptions—and, I confess, some misconceptions—about such issues as race, social change, and personal transformation. My editor, Allan Fallow, picked my brain and sutured my syntax, thus qualifying him for a doctor of rhetoric degree. Profound thanks are due, too, to David Halberstam for his thoughtful foreword and to Marian Wright Edelman for her inspiring afterword.

I am also deeply indebted to the editing talents of Carol Simons and Bill Newcott and the research assistance of Gretchen Gailey and Corinne Hayward. AARP attorney Michael Schuster provided invaluable counsel throughout, while AARP senior editor Karen Reyes secured releases at the 11th hour. Kudos to Carl Lehmann-Haupt for his original book design, as well as to AARP design director Eric Seidman and photo editors Linda Ferrer and Corinna Barsan of Creative Partners Ltd. in New York, all of whom worked tirelessly to give *My Soul* the right look. Without Marty Ittner—proprietor of the well-named "All-Night House o' Design"—the book never would have found its way to the printer on time. Production gurus Chris Boardwine and Mel Baughman troubleshot recalcitrant digital files.

There is no way to say a big enough thank you to AARP's Tom Nelson, Christine Donohoo, Dawn Sweeney, Cathy Ventura-Merkel, and Laura Rossman for their enthusiastic support of this book. They loved the idea from the outset and backed up their words with the resources to realize the project. A special note of appreciation to Steve Riggio, CEO of Barnes & Noble, without whose vision this book would never have been created. Thanks too to everyone at Sterling Publishing, notably Charles Nurnberg, Steven Magnuson, and Andrew Martin. The performance of Rena Kornbluh, Ronni Stolzenberg, Rick Willett, John Woodside, and Leigh Ann Ambrosi was sterling as well.

My most personal appreciation goes to my wife, Delise, who transforms so many lives every day as a child therapist. That may be why she believed so strongly in this book about transformation. On this book as on every other, Delise helped me focus on the main event and kept me organized with notes and ideas. When I felt overwhelmed and weighed down by pressure and uncertainty, Delise revived me with love and shots of confidence.

Special thanks go to my daughter Rae. On her way to law school she somehow found the time to read the manuscript and talk with me about its impact. My son Antonio, who loves to debate political theory, and my youngest son, Raphael, a keen mind and caring soul in one body, always had smart ideas and enthusiasm for this book.

I also want to thank my lawyer, Bob Barnett, for his passionate support. I am in debt to my friend Christopher Teal and his wife, Brook (as well as their son, Avery), for the long hours Chris spent discussing American social history with me. Divinity student Nora Campbell MacQueen expressed her social critic's interest in the motivation behind the people in these pages.

I also want to acknowledge my provocative friend Armstrong Williams and my supportive colleagues at National Public Radio, the Fox News Channel, *America's Black Forum*, and the American Program Bureau.

One powerful benefit of *My Soul Looks Back in Wonder*, I hope, will be its enduring value for young people. In these pages emerging leaders will find a road map to action. My prayer is that this book will inspire my children's generation to create with their hands, their feet, and their hearts the next great American story.

Juan Williams
*Washington, D.C.*
*March 2004*

SIX-YEAR-OLD RUBY BRIDGES enters William Frantz School in New Orleans in 1960, becoming the first African American child to desegregate an elementary school.

*Foreword*

# THE TRANSFORMING MOMENT

*By David Halberstam*

WE SHOULD BEGIN BY REMEMBERING America—not just the South—in that moment just before the Civil Rights Movement began. It was a time when, nearly a century after the Emancipation Proclamation, millions of Americans, through no fault of their own, had become the children of neo-slavery.

They were native sons and daughters, but they were completely disenfranchised in the land of the free and the home of the brave. They could not vote. They could not run for office. They could not serve on juries. They could not attend the great state universities that their dollars helped fund. They could not attend their own community's best public schools. They could not stay in local motels, eat in local restaurants, nor enter the local movie theaters by the main entrance and sit downstairs with all the other customers. They could not use the same water fountains or restrooms as whites in downtown civic buildings, including, most significantly, the local courthouse. All the powers of the state itself—its police power allied with its judicial power, with the federal government conveniently looking the other way—were used to suppress black people politically, educationally, socially, and economically, keeping them as marginally literate chattel—neither slaves nor citizens.

In town after town, they were denied the elemental dignity allotted all other citizens. If and when they were mentioned in local newspapers, they were not granted the basic honorifics—the use of "Mr." or "Miss" or "Mrs."—before their names. Anyone who wanted to—stranger or boss—could call them "nigger" to their faces without any recompense. Yet blacks had one great reminder of their citizenship: They were free to serve in the armed forces of their country.

The Civil Rights Movement changed all that. It was a largely peaceful revolution, but a revolution nonetheless. In my mind the movement spanned 10 years, from December 1955, when Rosa Parks refused to yield her seat on a bus in Montgomery, Alabama, and a young minister named Martin Luther King, Jr., became the head of a citywide bus boycott there, to August 1965, when Congress passed the Voting Rights Act. That bill gave blacks easy access with whites to political franchise in the South. No longer could a white registrar ask a potential black voter how many bubbles there were in a bar of Ivory Soap and exclude him from voting. The Voting Rights Act allowed blacks to vote for sheriffs and congressmen and district attorneys, placed blacks on juries, and ended state-sanctioned racism.

But it is also possible to chart the beginning of the movement to May 17, 1954, when the Supreme Court ruled unanimously in *Brown v. Topeka, Kansas Board of Education* that "separate educational facilities are inherently unequal." More change, legal and political, took place in those 11 years than in the previous 100.

This was nothing less than a great citizen's movement, harnessing the energies of blacks and whites alike. The first stage of the movement was led by well-educated, middle-class black ministers, skilled at taking the white man's Christianity—which had become their Christianity as well—and using it against him. The movement forced ordinary white citizens to examine their consciences, even as it summoned black people to reject the condition of their lives.

The second stage was something of a children's crusade as the students at black colleges began to drive it. That happened in 1960, when six long years after the *Brown* decision—and with no change apparent in their lives—they started the first sit-in demonstrations (lunch-counter protests) in Greensboro, North Carolina, and Nashville, Tennessee. A year later, they took it even farther, venturing into vastly more dangerous venues in the Deep South.

That historic demarcation point—when the students moved past the ministers—came in spring 1961. Some genteel middle-class protesters from the Congress of Racial Equality (CORE) headed out on Freedom

Rides, in which racially mixed bus passengers tested allegedly integrated facilities across the South, and were violently put down by the Klan. The senior ministerial leaders, stunned by the ferocity of the violence, wanted no part of additional Freedom Rides. But the student leadership represented by the Student Nonviolent Coordinating Committee (SNCC)—decided to resume them—to go ahead into Alabama—over the resistance of their great mentors, the black ministers.

The ministers, of course, were apprehensive about sending any young person on so dangerous a mission. Would they send their own children on it? That was the acid test. The answer was surely no. But the students, fresh from their victories in the sit-ins, felt differently. Student leader John Lewis, then only 21 and a Bible student at Nashville's American Baptist Theological Seminary, asked the ministers: "If not us, who?" Then he added, "If not now, when?"

When the ministers refused to finance the purchase of bus tickets, the students borrowed the money from a numbers man in Nashville. As they took the next courageous step—bringing the battle to the most recalcitrant parts of the South, what they called The Valley of the Shadow of Death—they had no protection from their enemies. I still think of them as being like the men who went

FREEDOM MARCHERS make their way from Selma to Montgomery, Alabama. By the time they reached the capital, March 25, 1965, they were 25,000 strong. Months later, President Lyndon Johnson signed the historic Voting Rights Act of 1965.

ashore at Normandy on D-Day in June 1944, except that they were doing this for their own rights on native soil and carried no weapons.

Their hope was, in the beginning, a fragile one: Wherever they went, it was clear to them by then, the media would go as well, and where the media went, the federal government, however reluctantly, would have to follow. And gradually that happened, even though President Kennedy was loath to challenge the powerful senior Southern congressional leadership of his own party and referred to the students at first as a "pain in the ass."

It was probably the best-run volunteer movement of modern times—and amazingly democratic. The people who signed on seemed to come together as much by accident as anything else; those pulled into it often had little inkling, as they first came aboard, of how much it would change not merely their country, but their own lives. Above all the Civil Rights Movement reflected a deep yearning on the part of ordinary people for a more just America. It was essentially a struggle to define the national conscience in a predominantly white, middle-class country—and, in the process, to undo the darkest chapter in American history: that of slavery. This was not just a test of the quality of life in Mississippi and Alabama, it became increasingly clear, but the ultimate test of the nature of democracy in America itself.

The movement created its own momentum: The greater the risks the young people took—and the more cruel and violent the resistance they encountered—the more the rest of the nation swung to their side. The cream of young Southern black students was met by bombs, guns, cattle prods, and attack dogs. As that happened, the rest of the nation often had to make choices it would just as soon not have made.

Why the movement exploded into being at this precise moment in American history is difficult to say. I believe two great forces jump-started it. The first was World War II—a war fought, as far as most Americans were concerned, not so much for complicated geopolitical reasons but rather between good and evil, between democracy and totalitarianism. To many Americans, that war was a crusade—but would the crusade for a more just world take place only on foreign soil? Would there be no continuum back home for those same ideals when the war was over? As such, World War II profoundly transformed the outlook of many of the young men who fought in it—they bought into its great themes, and they wanted to come back to a more just, more decent society when it was over. In addition, millions of blacks had served their country in the military; they were more confident now, and less willing to go back to the old segregated ways.

The second great factor was the rise of a powerful new media machine that subjected racism to withering new scrutiny. American journalism was on an upswing in the postwar years; newspapermen and women were—like their audience—more affluent and better educated. The *Brown* decision gave editors all over the country a green light to take a hard new look at race in the South. A year after *Brown*, when two white men murdered a black teenager named Emmett Till for allegedly whistling suggestively at one of their wives, the media convergence on the trial in Tallahatchie County, Mississippi, was unprecedented. Many young World War II veterans covered the civil rights beat in those days, and they were appalled to find their country mired in such dark racism.

But that was only a part of it. What became the crucial ingredient was a powerful new journalistic instrument called television. Rarely in journalistic history had there been a technological change that so dramatically altered the story itself. What killed state-sanctioned racism was bias—not the bias of journalists themselves, but the bias of the camera. Network news, then done in black and white, was in its infancy. The country was still being wired from coast to coast, and what the news desks needed was the legitimacy that came with covering so big, so important, so dramatic an event. The pictures told their own devastating story: Young American blacks, patiently and politely demanding the rights that all Americans took for granted, were being brutally beaten for their efforts. If the black leadership under men such as Martin Luther King, Jr., James Lawson, and Andrew Young had not anticipated the political sea change this new medium represented, it quickly understood its value. King in effect became a great tele-dramatist—and the nation watched this great morality play unfold before it nightly.

King and the men around him soon selected their protest venues based on the local authorities' potential for villainy. They badly needed men like Sheriff Jim Clark of Selma and Public Safety Commissioner Bull Connor of Birmingham. Those men in turn rarely let King down. In their own minds they were protecting a cherished birthright and a way of life handed down through many generations in their own families. Confident of the rectitude of their cause, they were applauded nightly by their closest friends for their show of integrity. To most Americans, however, it was the black protesters who were wearing the white hats. "All we wanted," Andrew Young told me as the movement gathered momentum during the 1960s, "was to reach the center of the nation, to affect the elderly white ladies in Iowa who voted for Senator Bourke Hickenlooper [a conservative Iowa Republican]."

In time, they did. The leadership of the movement lured the beast of segregation to the surface from the depths where it usually resided, revealing to the nation how racism worked and what price it exacted. In the process, these courageous men and women changed the conscience of the country, and in so doing they changed the nature of the United States government. It is important to remember that when the movement began, no part of the government—local, state or federal, save the Supreme Court—was on its side. Dwight Eisenhower, the president when the Court initially ruled, later referred to his choice of Earl Warren for Chief Justice as "the biggest damn fool mistake" he had ever made. (Warren had made sure that when the Court ruled in favor of *Brown*, it did so unanimously.)

In the South, all aspects of the government were aligned against the movement. Those venturing forth for change experienced a terrible loneliness. The FBI was headed by J. Edgar Hoover, an avowed racist who seemed more determined to find evidence of interracial sex among the protesters than to track down those who committed violent crimes against them. What turned the tide was the murder of three young protesters in the summer of 1964, one of them black (James Chaney) and two of them white (Andrew Goodman and Michael Schwerner). It was a brutal, vicious crime—an execution, really—carried out by the Klan and led by local law enforcement officers. It had happened as the three took part in a major campaign to register black voters.

The killings shocked the nation. That three young Americans had been murdered in the act of trying to help other Americans exercise the simplest democratic right—the right to vote—especially offended the

THE NEW MEDIUM of television delivers the face of segregation—Alabama Governor George Wallace—into homes nationwide in 1965. The civil rights drama made great TV, captivating—and transforming—the American public.

sitting President, Lyndon B. Johnson. A Southerner himself, Johnson told Hoover that he could stay on as FBI chief, but the charade was over; the FBI would have to switch sides and go after the Klan. That was the final increment of change in government. A year later, with Johnson pushing hard for it, the Voting Rights Act passed. The movement's great victory was the final step in ending state-sanctioned racism.

Fifty years after the *Brown* decision, the question remains: How much did it matter? The burden of race still weighs down much of American life, but the answer is easy: The gains from those years were enormous—a dramatic change often obscured because the road ahead remains so long, because so much damage was done in the previous 200 years. But in changing American life for the better, in starting the process of rescuing the nation from the cruelest part of its own history, the Civil Rights Movement is a glorious, luminescent, critically important chapter. It is American democracy at its very best.

AN IMMIGRANT FROM EL SALVADOR
shows his colors at a rally in
Washington, D.C., to raise awareness of
newcomers' struggle for equality.

*Introduction*

# THE SOUL OF CHANGE

THIS IS A BOOK ABOUT PERSONAL transformation. It is about new life through new sight, by which I mean insight. For some people, that insight comes in a flash of revelation. For others, it arrives like a slow dawn as understanding rises gradually to replace dark indifference.

As we open our eyes to the power of race in American society, we begin to perceive the impact of class and gender, too. Dropping the blinders reveals how often we heap disdain on the elderly, people with AIDS, people with little education. Seeing clearly is the first step in any individual's transformation.

Martin Luther King, Jr., often preached about the power of transformation. To a group of young people in a hurry to crush bigotry—perhaps even resorting to violence—he offered some startling counsel: "The nonviolent approach does not immediately change the heart of the oppressor. It first does something to the hearts and souls of those committed to it. It gives them new self-respect; it calls up resources of strength and courage that they did not know they had. Finally, it reaches the opponent and so stirs his conscience that reconciliation becomes a reality."

This book is a meditation on King's words. It is a compilation of narratives about coming to terms with conscience. These stories reflect the many voices and experiences of people who lived through the Civil Rights Movement and other struggles for equality, including the women's movement, the struggle for gay rights, and even the fight to save the environment.

The American idea is unique: creating one nation out of so many people of different racial and ethnic backgrounds, who speak different languages, who have different skin colors. It is an experiment in how these people, often facing brutal discrimination, stand up to ask for equal opportunity and make their contribution to American life.

At the heart of this drama is a personal struggle: how to deal with the fear engendered by living in a country with people from all over the world. Nor is that the only dilemma. Every American also has to figure out how to deal with people who are rich and poor; people who were born here and those who are newly arrived; people who are descendants of *Mayflower* passengers and those whose ancestors came here as slaves. There is no getting away from this quandary. With its promise of justice and equality for all, America presents a tremendous challenge. But each of us fashions a different answer to satisfy our soul. The story of how each one of us struggles to deal with "the other" is the great American adventure.

This book tells those stories. It is filled with inspiring examples of people who opened their eyes and their minds, then showed others the way. In these pages you will meet extraordinary individuals who tapped into their personal power to become agents of change. They are those rare souls who, through sacrifice and risk, dared take direct action to create a better America. They *are* American history.

Abraham Lincoln is a model. He had his first transformative experience on a trip to New Orleans as a little boy. His father took young Abe to the docks to see black people—some of them stripped naked—sold as slaves. The boy witnessed children torn from their parents as mere business transactions among white men regarded as upstanding citizens of the day.

That experience left a deep emotional scar. By Lincoln's own admission, he did not then view blacks as equal to whites. But black slaves were human beings, he concluded, and they deserved the right to live as free people. That realization led Lincoln to argue against slavery as an adult—and later, as President, to author the Emancipation Proclamation.

The best of American history is made up of people like Lincoln who experience a moment of revelation that inspires them to fight against injustice. No matter how momentous the issue, social transformation begins with individuals awakening to a new way of seeing the world.

### THE ORANGE AND THE BLACKJACK GAME

In 1954 the Supreme Court made a landmark decision—*Brown v. Topeka, Kansas Board of Education*—that ended legal segregation of public schools and changed forever the nation's legal, political, and cultural life. As school doors slowly opened across the country, more blacks, Hispanics, and Asians graduated from high school and college than ever before. With education came higher earning power and added political clout. As a result, the nation now has the largest black and Hispanic middle class in history—and an unprecedented number of minority leaders in city halls, state legislatures, and the U.S. Congress.

Many people helped move the *Brown* decision forward, but one man carried the ball across the goal line: Thurgood Marshall, the head of the NAACP Legal Defense Fund, who later became the nation's first black Supreme Court justice. Marshall grew up in Baltimore, Maryland, where he attended segregated schools and rode segregated public transportation. But his early experience with segregation left him neither angry nor defiant. That would come later, after a simple but profound moment of transformation convinced him that integration—particularly in education—was essential for the full promise of democracy.

In the summer of 1933, newly graduated from Howard University Law School, Marshall took a trip through the South with his law school dean and mentor, Charles Hamilton Houston, to evaluate the differences between black and white elementary schools. Not surprisingly, they found that the white schools usually had new books, ample classrooms, cafeterias, and school buses; the black schools were often small and cramped, with torn, hand-me-down books and makeshift supplies.

At one of the schools, Marshall stood outside eating his lunch when an eight-year-old black boy approached him, staring at the food. The boy was riveted by an orange sitting on the hood of the car, so Marshall handed it to the boy—who bit directly into the rind. Surprised at the bitter taste, he spit it out. Then the boy touched his eye, and the sting prompted him to throw the orange on the ground.

Marshall began swearing at the boy for wasting the orange. Houston rushed over. The poor child had never seen an orange before, he explained. What could he know of peeling it, much less separating its slices or picking out the seeds?

Marshall was stunned. That night he wrote his mother a letter in which he vowed to represent the poor, ill-educated black children of the South, their lives so circumscribed they didn't even know what an orange was. "A lawyer who is not a social engineer is nothing but a social parasite," Houston had once told Marshall, but those words lacked meaning for him until the boy brought them to life. Now Marshall had a mission that would eventually lead him to engineer the NAACP's victory in the *Brown* case.

Marshall's successor on the high court, Clarence Thomas, experienced a similar epiphany—yet he emerged from it as a conservative activist rather than a liberal one, often vilified for refusing to adopt the official positions of prominent African Americans. Instead, Thomas remains loyal to his own thinking, including his opposition to affirmative action.

Years before he became a Supreme Court justice, Thomas told me that his convictions had begun to crystallize when he was the only black student at a seminary high school. Thomas got good grades, but he felt isolated; he had to tolerate frequent racial jokes. He felt defined by his skin color. This realization led to his lifelong effort to run counter to stereotype, his refusal to be pigeonholed intellectually simply because he was black.

Thomas reached back to a moment in his Georgia boyhood to elaborate. He had been on a porch playing blackjack for pennies with some friends. One boy was winning most hands. Watching him closely, Thomas realized that he had marked the cards. When Thomas called him on his cheating, a fight erupted. Amid the shouting, everyone grabbed for the money on the table. In the aftermath, there was no way to untangle the cheating and divide the money fairly; not everyone had cheated. Yet everyone still wanted to play. So Thomas and his friends—the cheater included—promised not to cheat, and the game resumed. They allowed the money to remain in the fast hands of whoever had grabbed it first.

To Thomas, that story reflects the history of race relations in

TURNING POINT: Martin Luther King, Jr., is greeted by wife Coretta in 1956 after leaving Montgomery, Alabama, court. He was convicted of conspiracy to boycott city buses; the judge suspended his fine. The case put King into the national spotlight.

America. Whites used slavery and segregation to cheat blacks. But there is no way, he argues, to repair the damage done to ex-slaves who are dead or people who lost opportunities because of racial bias. The best solution was to start over and be more vigilant. He wouldn't cheat because he had been cheated. Instead, he had to play with more skill and protect himself. It was a transforming moment for Thomas that continues to guide his thinking about race on the Supreme Court.

### MEETINGS WITH REMARKABLE MEN

The story of transformation is not limited to the American experience. It is universal.

In 1990 I went to South Africa as a *Washington Post* correspondent to cover Nelson Mandela's historic release from prison. One night I found myself at his dinner table in Soweto as he celebrated with friends and relatives he hadn't seen in 27 years. Over a home-cooked South African stew, I asked him if he'd wanted to break apart the apartheid system even as a child.

Mandela, a serious man, laughed.

The only rebellion in his heart as a young man, he said, had been his desire to rebel against his parents. He wanted to leave home for the big city, Johannesburg, get an education, learn to box, study poetry and the law. Only when he learned that he couldn't represent his legal clients properly did he become active with the African National Congress. And when he began to speak out against apartheid, he suddenly realized that he had an opportunity to inspire a nation. This was not only a turning point for Mandela, it was a turning point for South Africa and the rest of the world.

Later on that trip, I too had a moment of transformation.

I met Zephania Mothopeng, head of South Africa's Pan-African Party. A thin, blind man then in his late 80s, he sat smiling but unmoving in a chair near his bed as we talked. A small radio played religious music in the background. Before I could start interviewing him, Mothopeng began to interview me. He was curious about a young black man from so far away.

"Do you know what country you are visiting?"

"South Africa," I replied.

"No such place exists," Mothopeng informed me. "That is a name white settlers gave to land long held and named by various black African tribes."

As I listened to Mothopeng speak, I felt as if he were addressing the child in me. That child had long struggled with difficult and personal questions. Why are so many black and brown people in this world so poor and ill-educated? Why do black and brown people fill American jails in such disproportionate numbers?

At the time of the interview I was 36 years old and successfully middle class, but I had grown up in a poor section of Brooklyn. My father trained boxers and did bookkeeping to supplement his income. My mother sewed dresses and later worked as a secretary. Neither had a high school education. We never owned an automobile. So that my older sister could go to high school in the United States, my father had sent my mother and three children, including 3-year-old me, from Panama to New York City. Our first apartment had only one bedroom, which meant my brother and I had to sleep in the living room. We had a radio but no TV and my brother got mad at me when my Aunt Annie, who had a TV, would invite me over to her apartment to spend the night. Five years later my father joined the family and we moved to a sparsely furnished two-bedroom apartment on Bedford Avenue.

I told Mothopeng none of this, but as he talked my mind scanned past memories of racial tension in Brooklyn. When my family moved into Crown Heights, a neighborhood in transition, you could sense the whites' fear of black people. They steadily left the neighborhood, and their children left the schools. At my schools—P.S. 241 and Lefferts Junior High—the top students were mostly white, even though the student body had become mostly black. After-school fights usually involved the black kids on the lowest academic track, called C.G. for Career Guidance or vocational training. And when the police arrived, they often led away poor black kids.

I could see the predominant white attitude in my schoolbooks. History texts either didn't mention black people or mentioned them in passing as primitives and slaves. On television, in movies, and in newspapers, white affluence and power and celebrations of white beauty abounded. I didn't have to be told as a child that whites viewed blacks as a scourge. I could see it everywhere in action.

ON THE THRESHOLD OF JUSTICE: Thurgood Marshall *(center)* celebrates the U.S. Supreme Court's *Brown v. Board of Education* decision with fellow lawyers George Hayes *(left)* and James Nabrit on May 17, 1954.

How could I explain this to Mothopeng, who had lived through years of violent oppression in South Africa? How could I explain a nation that talks about democratic ideals and racial justice but where only white people had nice houses and political power? Would he think I was an overly sensitive punk if I told him how my chest tightened when my mother told me that her boss at the garment factory wouldn't let her go to the bathroom except during official breaks, even when she was sick? The boss was white and all the workers were black. No one dared challenge him for fear of losing her job. And what would Mothopeng think about my schools? Racially segregated or not, even ghetto schools in the United States are far better than the schools available to most black South African children.

It would have been too much to explain to Mothopeng the subtle—and sometimes not-so-subtle—advantages that white children had at school and how those inequities had led me to doubt myself, my intellect, my future. If the bosses are white, the president and mayor are white, the teachers are white, and most of the top students are white, what does that say about black people? What does it say about me, a black man? Are black people inferior to all white people?

I hated this logic. I both envied and resented the outward signs of wealth and power in a white majority country. In public-opinion polls, many Americans view blacks and Hispanics as more likely to be "somewhat lazy and violence prone." A 1988 poll found that more than one-third of whites thought that "blacks tend to have less ambition than whites." And a 1978 poll found that about one-fourth of whites agreed that blacks have less intelligence than whites. These barriers of perception are as real as any jail cell that imprisons the human spirit.

My aunt used to say that God had created a rainbow of colors; if we were all the same color there would be nothing to see—and we might as well all be blind. I took it as cold comfort in a world where people of color were clearly regarded as inferior. I could see the reality of black poverty and despair every day in my neighborhood. Even when my mother spoke bitterly of the bigotry of whites, I had to wonder if whites did not have some claim to their feelings of superiority because of the wealth and power they commanded. As I grew up and felt the sting of racist assumptions about my intellect—or the shame of being called a "darky"—my feelings about race relations became tinged with anger. But beneath it all, as I sat there in South Africa as a journalist for a major American newspaper, was the child's question of why whites had more money, more power, and more prominence in the history books.

All of this was fresh in my mind as Mothopeng described the tactics of racial domination in South Africa. At one point, he leaned toward me and asked if I understood what happened when black farmers in South Africa had their land taken. They were forced to leave their families and go to work in the mines. Then he asked if I understood what happened when black children were given inferior schools that prepared them only for work in those mines or as servants, but nothing more. He didn't wait for an answer. Such oppressive practices, he said, had led to black South Africans' being disparaged as stupid, dirty, lazy, and morally inferior for failing to build strong families.

As Mothopeng spoke, he opened a window of understanding for the child in me who had wrestled with the conflict between black pride and the black struggle for survival in America. I had read about the evils of colonialism, but I lived in a time of freedom movements and black breakthroughs in business, culture, and the arts. I was focused on the future to the point of intentionally closing my eyes to the pain of the past. I had never thought of the black people I knew best—in the United States, the Caribbean, and South America—as so thoroughly exploited. But as Mothopeng spoke to me, I experienced a moment of grace—a moment in which the damage done by colonialists and slave traders assumed a sudden immediacy. And I could understand its grip across generations of black families, even those focused on achievement despite the burden of racism.

The African leader's insistent questioning nudged me toward a new view of race and a new view of myself. All the negative stereotypes of violence, anger, intellectual weakness, and criminality jelled into an awareness of the consequences of a people repeatedly pushed to the periphery of society. The sense of striving to escape stereotypes, to break free of the prison of low expectations, was supplanted in my mind by an awareness of where I fit in the historical arc of racial indignities and injustices spanning continents and centuries. It made me proud to think that black people had resisted degradation and insisted on their own inherent dignity in the face of such assaults on their sense of personal worth.

### THE POWER OF ONE

This is not just a black-and-white story. It embraces all of us. It is the story of the human spirit rising to embrace a vision of a world in which men and women of all races are free to be themselves.

Elizabeth Cady Stanton and Lucretia Mott are two famous examples. They gained a sense of their own power trying to abolish slavery in the early 1800s. That experience transformed them from reserved, unassuming women to daring, outspoken leaders who gave birth to the women's suffragist movement. In 1848 Stanton and Mott convened the Seneca Falls Women's Rights Convention, the first meeting of its kind. The movement they started that day led to passage of the 19th Amendment, which in 1920 gave women the right to vote. Stanton and Mott had a vision that has fueled the women's movement for over 150 years and continues to empower women of all ages.

César Chávez had a similar breakthrough. Angry at the discrimination he faced as a migrant worker, he envisioned a way for low-paid grape pickers in California to take power and create a better life for themselves. Working with Dolores Huerta in 1962, Chávez founded the National Farm Workers Association, then organized a campaign to encourage consumers to boycott grapes in support of economic justice for migrant laborers. His innovative nonviolent tactics included fasting to get media attention and a mass march from the grape fields of Delano, California, to the state capitol in Sacramento in 1966 carrying a banner reading *VIVA LA CAUSA!* (LONG LIVE OUR CAUSE!).

Many gay Americans changed the way they viewed themselves in 1969 when the Stonewall Riots erupted in New York City. The idea that gays and lesbians—long accustomed to living in secrecy, even shame—could stand up for their rights was a shock to many in the closeted gay community. That incident led Ron Gold, Barbara Gittings, and others to create the National Gay and Lesbian Task Force in 1973, transforming the anger of Stonewall into positive action that put gay rights front and center in the national consciousness.

America is a land of people reinventing themselves. The little girl at the drugstore becomes a movie star; the high school dropout becomes a corporate kingpin. In almost every case, the new identity hinges on smashing stereotypes and prejudice to succeed.

In the late 1980s I traveled to New Mexico to examine the impact of voting rights on Native Americans. Farmington, in northwest New Mexico, was a town known for tense relations between whites and Native Americans. The town's economy was based on the coal-, gas-, and oil-drilling rights to land on Indian reservations. The whites resented the Indians, who they felt had not earned the right to the property but had received it as a gift from the federal government. Many local whites also spoke bitterly about the tax exemptions and welfare payments that the tribe had received along with treaties and land-use agreements. A white waitress told me: "Indians spend money like I spend money, only I earn my money—I get out and work for it."

The white disdain for Native Americans produced a shocking crime. In 1974, three drunk Navajo men in Farmington had been beaten, set on fire, and had their fingers chopped off by a group of white teenage boys. The killings set off demonstrations and calls by Native American leaders for an investigation. Indians had become accustomed to living with the fear of violence by whites in the Farmington area. Not until 1948 had they been allowed to vote in state or county elections—and even then, few challenged the traditional white control of politics. Only 10 percent of New Mexico's Indians were registered to vote in 1975.

The brutal deaths of the three Navajos transformed the Native American population into activists with a cause. The National Indian Youth Council went to court to end at-large elections. With the Indian population concentrated on reservations, Native American candidates found it difficult to win countywide races; white voters far outnumbered their American Indian counterparts. A court order finally established two voting districts where Native Americans lived so that they could elect their own political representatives.

Navajo Lynda Eaton joined those marches in 1978 and—for the first time in her life—raised her voice to demand justice. Ten years later, she resolved to make it easier for her fellow Navajos to reach San Juan Community College in Farmington, some 40 to 80 miles away from the two reservations where most of the Native Americans lived. That school was the only one that offered local Indians post-high school job training or an academic degree.

The school refused to budget money for a bus. The school lacked not only dorms but also had no Native Americans on its faculty and no Native American history courses in its curriculum. The heart of the problem? No Navajos served on San Juan College's five-member board of regents. In fact, no Navajos had ever run for the board.

As a child, Lynda Eaton had been warned by her parents never to visit Farmington alone. They told her that Indian girls were often attacked, even killed, by whites. So when San Juan school officials refused to build a dorm for Native Americans or provide them with transportation to the college, Eaton broke out of the normally silent stand of Navajo women. She rallied the support of tribal leaders and ran for the board of regents. Eaton spearheaded a drive that more than doubled the registration of Navajo voters in the vicinity. And she won a seat on the San Juan Community College's board of regents.

"Fifteen years ago," Eaton told me, "most Indians here were not aware that I had the right to run for office. They didn't even know if they would be allowed to register to vote. It's really pretty simple: Because we are voters now, whites are becoming aware that we are citizens. We vote,

JUBILATION REIGNS around South African leader Nelson Mandela after his release from prison in 1990. Mandela's turning point: Upon starting to speak out against apartheid, he discovered the power of nonviolence.

therefore we exist." Within two years, Eaton succeeded in securing funding for a fleet of shuttle buses between the two reservations and the community college; Indian enrollment at the school more than doubled in the first year the buses were in operation. Lynda Eaton—once a timorous teenager—had transformed herself into a force for change.

### ALL IN THE FAMILY

This kind of story is being repeated every day all over the United States—and all over the world.

My grandfather died while building the Panama Canal. As he stood in that tropical heat and mud taking his last breath, his imagination could extend only so far. What might he have envisioned for his son?

My father, standing on a street corner in Jamaica (where he was born in 1902), could never have imagined himself leaving his home and moving to the United States, where he and his children would find opportunities beyond his most fanciful dreams. Nor could he have ever imagined me, standing on a street corner today in Washington, D.C., as an author, reporter, and radio and TV personality with a job that allows me to help shape public opinion and go head to head with some of the nation's most powerful leaders.

And what about the fourth generation—my children? Already I see them probing the boundaries of possibility as they pursue directions in their lives inconceivable to me as a child in Brooklyn.

All of this is magic—yet what sorcerer could conjure such amazing transformations? Call it the everyday magic of the family: Each of us begins the journey toward personal discovery because someone else gave us a vision that allows us to be more creative, more resourceful, more powerful than the child inside us ever thought possible.

The pattern of one person awakening, sharing, and organizing is key to positive social change. It is the story of the American Revolution, the battle to abolish slavery, the fight to secure for women the right to vote. Technology and economics may appear to trigger most societal change, but most often the shift begins with an individual; he or she touches someone who then takes an action that, no matter how slight it seems, builds inexorably into a grand movement of people.

Prepare to witness such miracles in the pages that follow.

MAMIE TILL BRADLEY COLLAPSES upon glimpsing the open casket of her son, 14-year-old Emmett Till, beaten and shot dead on August 28, 1955, for the sin of whistling at a white woman in Mississippi.

# I

# THE WEIGHT

*"I look at the past and I see myself."*

**Miriam Makeba**

CHAPTER 1

# I AM A MAN

*Jesse Epps's family left Mississippi when he was a boy. Having witnessed racial violence, Jesse and his father worried that their family might be next.*

*Epps grew up to become the only black worker at a General Electric plant in Syracuse, New York. When he took the lead in organizing a labor grievance at the plant, his successful leadership attracted the attention of the International Union of Electrical Workers (IUEW). Later he joined the American Federation of State, County & Municipal Employees (AFSCME), and as a 32-year-old labor official was sent to Memphis to help with the 1968 sanitation workers' strike. It came to be known as the "I Am a Man" campaign, and drew Martin Luther King, Jr., for his last, fateful journey.*

MY DAD TAUGHT US GROWING up that no man was any better than any other man. We recognized that Mississippi in those days was not a part of the United States of America.

What got my attention that things needed to change happened one day in Dublin, Mississippi, in 1948, when I was 12.

Dublin was built along the railroad tracks and had a little town square with all the main stores. White folks lived on one side of the tracks and black folks lived on the other. So we had demarcation of the community.

The square had a canopy over it, and there was the "loafers' bench" where people could sit and congregate. You could walk across to the post office, which was built on the other side of the tracks—the black side. Every Saturday the rich town boss would walk over to the post office, get his mail, and go back home.

On one occasion there was a black man—God bless his heart, I know not his name—but the rich white town boss approached with his two daughters up the sidewalk, and the black man didn't stop for him. All the rest of the folks were looking as to what he was going to do. The white boss got within 10 feet of this black man and addressed him: "Nigger, get off the sidewalk!"

The black man stood there. The third time he addressed him, the rich white man said, "Do you know who I am?"

And the black man said, yes, he knew who he was, but he didn't see getting off the sidewalk and into the street to let him pass. He said, "This sidewalk looks big enough for both of us."

The town boss did not say a word. He turned around and took his daughters with him and went back to his house, got his gun and came

back and shot the black man, and kicked his body off the sidewalk into the gutter. He then dragged the body into the street and called the sheriff. And nothing was ever done about it.

I didn't know how to forgive my dad for being one of the men who watched that and took no action. But he was wiser than I was. I said if I ever get the opportunity, I would do something.

Integrated busing was not an issue, because we walked to school and the white kids were bused to school, half of them along muddy roads. On rainy days, we had to jump in the ditch to get out of the way of the bus. If we didn't, the driver would deliberately splash water on us as he passed by.

Since our father operated a small farm, we were not exposed

STRIKING SANITATION WORKERS assemble in Memphis, Tennessee, on March 28, 1968, with thousands of civil rights activists for the "I AM A MAN" protest, which Jesse Epps helped organize. It would be Dr. King's last march.

to a total plantation environment. I had eight brothers and six sisters, and we were taught some basic principles growing up: Love of God and respect for our neighbors without regard to race. When you met a person along the way, speak to a lady, tip your hat. So the white folks loved that—they thought, "That young man is very respectful"—but we did it to the black folks too. My father taught us to say, "Yes, sir"—not "Yassuh"—to every adult, black or white. He said you treat black folks and white folks one and the same.

What persuaded my dad to move the family away was after my brothers and I had an altercation with a group of white boys. We had gone to Dublin one day, and decided to take a shortcut home by cutting across the field on a plantation owned by a white family. The shortcut saved us two and a half miles of walking to our property.

There was also a family of white tenants, sharecroppers, living on the property, and they had kids our age. The white sharecropper kids decided they were going to give us whatever for coming across their land.

A fight started, and they got surprised. We sent them scurrying and went on home.

My dad was in the village later and he heard that the white people were going to come down to our little house that night and teach us a lesson. Dad came home quickly and told us to get up in the loft because the white people were going to come. We all had a gun and he had taught us to shoot it.

Our little farm was set back about half a mile off the road. My dad ordered us to circle the wagons. All of us took up our spots with our guns around the house.

Then my dad went back into town and told the sheriff what had happened. He said if they came that night there was going to be a slaughter of white folks on his property. He returned to the house and we waited.

Just about dusk, we saw a car turning into our road and we figured, "Here they come!" We were all armed, and there was enough of us to put up a fight.

When the car got closer, we saw it was the sheriff. He drove up, got out, and told my dad, "Charlie, I talked to those fellers and you don't have to worry about anything happening tonight. Those boys had no business bothering your boys. I made them understand you have always raised your kids up to be respectful."

Dad said, "Okay," and the sheriff drove off. But we sat there all during the night anyway. And of course they never came.

After that event, Dad decided it was better to get out of Mississippi.

Years later I was sent to Memphis to help Theo Jones, who was trying to organize the sanitation workers there. They worked 12 hours a day carrying garbage with busted, leaking pails. Some were infested with flies and maggots, and they had no place to wash up in the yard where they had to leave the trucks. They had no running water in their homes when they got home. And of course no real benefits of any kind.

When I arrived in Memphis, we had no place to meet. All the churches I asked wouldn't help, nor would any of the other unions. So I called up the international president of the United Auto Workers; they had a nice large meeting hall, and they let us use that. And the Rev. Malcolm Blackburn, the pastor of Clayburn Temple Church who happened to be white, opened his heart and his church to the sanitation men.

During this period we were trying to find something we could put on a sign that could say it all. It must have been almost midnight, and we'd been struggling, and we had a sign that said "I AM A MAN." It was God's inspiration. With that sign we changed the idea that these garbage workers were gluttons making unfair demands. It was clear that these were men whose dignity and respect and manhood was being preyed upon.

In the end, close to 1,400 men joined the strike, and they shut the city down.

On his first visit to Memphis, King spoke to a crowd of 17,000 and called for a citywide march.

When we first asked Dr. King to come speak to the garbage workers, his reaction was, "We don't get involved in labor disputes."

Dr. King said to me, "I sympathize and understand the problems, Jesse, but my plate is full." He was running all over the country trying to create some excitement for the Poor People's Campaign. He said, "You know, I'm up against the wall, and I really can't come down, because I cannot abandon this project."

I told him, "We're not asking you to abandon it. We're saying that this is very much a part of it. So you cannot afford to pass by these men." The Rev. Jim Lawson, who had pioneered the movement's use of nonviolent techniques, finally got Dr. King to agree to come. When he came, he saw the real fervor of what was going on here, and it energized him.

During the time we were trying to resolve the strike, I bought some traps and we caught a bunch of rats from the homes of our members. Then we held a press conference and I showed the rats and talked again about the deplorable conditions of the men at work. I announced that the union was going to buy me 100 to 200 traps, and what we would do—since we were humanitarians—was turn them loose out in East Memphis.

All the white folks, they were ready to tar and feather me. The next day, I was told, many of the supply houses sold out of rat traps.

That focused the attention of the folks who thought they could ostracize labor. A couple of priests and the leadership in the white community reached out to us and wanted to know what they could do: "What is the real problem?"

They organized a group of women—wives of the clergy and the councilmen and businessmen in the community—and took them on a tour of the sanitation men's homes. Some of them wept. When that group of women saw firsthand how those men were living, things changed. The next day, the women went to City Hall and demanded that something be done for these men.

After King's death, President Johnson sent the Undersecretary of Labor down here to settle the strike. I guess I'll never know: Did that action make them change, or did they really think I was going to catch rats and throw them out there?

CHAPTER 2

# A DREAM IS A GOOD PLACE TO START

*Endesha Ida Mae Holland can look through the trees outside her second-floor room in Santa Monica, California, and see the Pacific Ocean. But simply by closing her eyes, she can see the events of her life—the tragedy and triumph, the horror and delight—rising and falling in lockstep with the past 60 years of the Civil Rights Movement.*

*Weak from a lifetime of beatings and the disease ataxia, Dr. Holland has chronicled her life's voyage in her book,* From the Mississippi Delta *(Simon & Schuster, 1997). Born in Greenwood, Mississippi, in 1944, she was the third of Ida Mae Garner's four children. Her mother supported her family by taking in laundry and renting out rooms by the day, the week ... and the hour.*

*Among Dr. Holland's earliest memories is that of hunting down cockroaches, then selling them to bait stores for use by local white fishermen.*

WE WEREN'T PROUD OF HAVING roaches, but we were kind of proud that they helped hook the bass and catfish that ended up battered and fried on white supper tables. It was a funny kind of line that connected the roaches to the fish, the blacks to the whites and my neighborhood to the rest of the world.

My mama was a midwife for local black women, and she got so good at catching babies that a white doctor helped her get her license—even though she couldn't read or write. I was just a child, but I helped by filling out birth certificates for her.

Mama was living her dream. She rushed around town to the sides of women in labor, wearing her clean white starched dress and cap, just like a nurse, toting a bulging black bag, just like a doctor. On a string around her neck she wore her nature sack, full of herbs. Gently but firmly, she'd tell a woman what to do. Mama's hands would roam over her stomach and read the signs as she reached inside to feel the baby and see how it was sitting. Her hands would tell her everything she needed to know. Mama had magic hands.

"Don'cha never gi'e your own dream up," she'd tell me. "You gotta start somewhere, an' a dream is jest as good a place as any!" From Mama's dream, I learned to dream, too—big and unafraid, no matter what obstacles or bitterness were put in my way.

The obstacles and bitterness began early. On my 11th birthday, I was invited to the home of Mr. and Mrs. Lawrence, a white family Mama did washing and ironing for. I thought I was there to play with their granddaughter. But soon Mrs. Lawrence told me that her husband wanted to see me upstairs to give me a birthday present. There I found Mr. Lawrence naked in bed. I can still feel the arms of Mrs. Lawrence, lifting me off my feet and into the arms of her husband.

When that old man had finished with me, he handed me a crumpled five-dollar bill and mumbled something I don't remember or didn't hear. "Happy birthday," maybe.

In the South, I was often told, no white man wanted to die without having sex with a black woman. It was just seen as a part of life. If you were white, only God had power over your life. But if you were black, you were always at the mercy of white people, and all you had in life was the hope of heaven.

I started hanging out with some of the older kids from school at local juke joints. With my woman-sized body, it was fairly simple to talk my way in, even though the owners knew I was underage.

Soon I was expelled from my school and my church. They said I was a prostitute. To the older generation, "streetwalking" meant prostitution. But to us younger women, streetwalking was another thing entirely. It was about strolling, trolling, and strutting your stuff, showing off from table to table in the juke joints. Your stride was your signature. Streetwalking girls might have sex, or they might not, and everyone knew it was their choice. A man's job was to entice them—

with drinks, flattery, slick manners, and tall talk—to make that choice their way. Merely trading sex for money—that was what whores and hookers did.

Despite my playing around, there was still a part of me that wanted respectability. And I thought I had found it with a man named Ike. He was from Rome, Mississippi, and worked for a butane gas company. He wore a starched uniform and drove a late-model green Chevrolet. He was also the first man to treat me like a lady.

Before long we were a couple, and the whole community accepted us as one. Mama loved Ike, not just because he kept her supplied with RC Cola and Garrett Snuff, but because he seemed like a good man with a good job. "Don't mess this one up, Cat!" she said. Even when I discovered I was pregnant, and I thought he'd leave me, he seemed delighted. But by the time our son Cedric was born, Ike had taken up with another woman. I moved back in with Mama—and went back to streetwalking, just to support my child.

One day a fine-looking newcomer caught my eye. His name was Robert Moses, and he was a tall, handsome math teacher who came down from Harlem. I started following him around, figuring he'd be a gentleman who'd want to spend some money on me.

I found out he was in town as director of a civil rights group called COFO (Council of Federated Organizations). With him were a dozen or so workers. People started calling them Moses and His Twelve Disciples.

I was standing with some friends outside his headquarters—they called it Freedom House—when he came to the door and said, "We need help to get people signed up. Who can read and write?" His voice was cool and deep—like Ike's without the jazz, but dressed up with education. And he was looking directly at me.

"G'won, Cat," my friend Miss Nonnie said, pushing me forward. Then she spoke up to Mr. Moses. "Dis 'un kin read an' write real good—her make out all my chilluns' birth 'tificates!"

Nobody else stepped forward. But if life had taught me nothing else, it had taught me to recognize a cue to get on stage. I followed him into Freedom House ... and I never came out.

I guess I became one of the leaders there in town. As things got violent, as the authorities resisted the Civil Rights Movement,

I always seemed to be one of the first to meet the police dogs and the billy clubs. We all spent a good amount of time in jail, and my experience in there gave me a leg up on those poor kids from the North, who knew nothing about this peculiar form of Southern hospitality.

A number of my past tricks, even the white men, gave me money—not for services rendered, but out of friendship and respect for my work in the movement. They kept it all very quiet, of course. Years later in New York City, for example, a young white man from Greenwood came up to me and apologized. He felt bad that his father, who was a local doctor, had done nothing to help us during the movement. I told him he didn't know what he was talking about. I told him that his father had helped smuggle supplies for us into Freedom House. He was both surprised and delighted. But you know, I think the other white people in town knew that doctor had been one of my customers. When he died they buried him in a plot beside the road, which in the South is a sign of disrespect.

As my work in the movement continued, I found I'd earned a kind of respect in the black community that I'd never imagined. When a bunch of us returned home after 33 days at maximum-security Parchman Penitentiary for marching without a permit—where they'd shaved our heads—we got a hero's welcome. Our bus pulled up in front of the Turner Chapel AME Church and we filed off, moving through the crowd and shaking everyone's hands, getting hugged and patted on the back like a football team returning from a championship win.

Mama was there in her wheelchair, and she hugged me and rubbed my stubbly head, saying "C'mere, ol' nappy-head gal!" I hugged her back until it hurt.

One of the greatest moments in Mama's life was the day Dr. Martin Luther King visited Greenwood. It was just after President Kennedy was killed, and I was accompanying Dr. King on a walking tour of our neighborhood. After greeting a couple of neighbors, we eased to the south side of the street, to our house, and Dr. King climbed the steps. He was in shirt-sleeves now, his jacket thrown over his shoulder. He extended his hand to Mama.

"How do you feel today, Miss Ida Mae?" Dr. King asked with a smile.

CROSS BURNINGS like this one—clandestinely photographed at a 1951 KKK gathering in South Carolina—spread terror to blacks and civil rights workers who dared to challenge the status quo in the South.

Mama smiled back politely, eyes big as cabbages, magnified behind her glasses, and shook his hand. "I be feeling' toler'ble well deday, Reverend Kang," she responded.

Dr. King turned to one of his traveling party like there was something important he forgot. "Bernard, why don't you go to the store over there and get Miss Ida Mae some ice cream, some RCs, and a container of Garrett Snuff?"

"Lawd amercy!" Mama slapped her cheeks, thrilled as all get out. "Y'all c'mere an' rest yo'self, Pastor Kang!"

For Mama, it was a dream come true—not only to meet Dr. King, but to see her daughter, the one who had once walked the streets, now walking with greatness.

And I realized I belonged there. In the following months I traveled through the North, raising money for the movement. On the campus of the University of Minnesota, I saw how black people could live with dignity—and vowed that I would return to study there some day.

There was a change in the community back in Greenwood, too. People who hadn't set foot in school for decades now crammed Mr. Moses' Freedom Schools. Black men who had never looked a white woman in the face now stood toe-to-toe with the registrar and argued for their rights. All over town, black and white civil rights workers broke bread together, watching and learning and laughing with each other. We saw black men walking hand in hand with white girls. We got used to hearing ourselves introduced as "Mr." and "Miss."

It was just a matter of time, I guess, before the backlash came. For me and Mama, it came early one morning in February 1965. My mother shook me awake and said, "Ida Mae! Ida Mae! Wake up, gal, an' lissen! Dem dogs," she said. "Lissen how dey be barkin'!" It was a rhythmic, unearthly howl. Nothing seemed wrong, exactly—but then again, things didn't seem quite right.

Mama had sent Cedric to the store to get some snuff. I went out on the front porch and saw Ike's car pulling into an alley, so I ran off looking for him. A few minutes later I saw the sky turn black, then I heard an explosion. I knew it was my house.

I ran back home and found the house in flames. A large ball of fire floated across our yard toward the rose bush by the steps. The ball rolled over and turned into Mama.

Somebody with a powerful hate in their heart had burned my Mama to death. They were after me, but they got my mama.

After that, I had to leave Greenwood. I remembered my vow on the University of Minnesota campus, and decided to make good on it. I left Cedric in the care of Ike's mother, and headed north, where he joined me later on. It took me 13 years, but in 1979 I finally got my Bachelor of Arts degree in African American Studies.

Black nationalist Maulana Ron Karenga spoke at the university and gave me the name "Endesha" in 1983. That's Swahili for "she who drives herself and others."

I stayed on for another five years, and in 1985—twenty years after leaving the Mississippi Delta—I received my Ph.D. in American studies.

CHAPTER 3

# KING OF THE BLUES

*With a storied career spanning seven decades, Riley B. King—B. B. King—is the undisputed master of the blues, the musical style rooted in slave songs. He grew up on a cotton plantation in the Mississippi Delta. Despite the pervasive backdrop of racial oppression, King has over the years purposefully shaped a kind of color-blind blues.*

*Resplendent in a formal tuxedo and fighting off a bad case of the flu, the 78-year-old King sat in the back of his touring bus just before taking the stage for another sold-out show, recalling what life was like for him as a child.*

MY FATHER WAS FROM THE flatlands around Indianola, Mississippi. We call it the Delta. My mother went down there to visit someone; met my dad and they fell in love, got married. And they say, you know, here is me.

They lived together until I was about five, and then they divorced. My mother then went back to what we call the Hill Country. She died when I was nine, and my grandmother—her mother—died the next year, so that left me kind of by myself.

During that time they didn't have the laws as they do today, where certain people would have places for orphans and so on. They didn't have that in the country. Everybody was sort of like your guardian. You had to walk the straight and narrow, because anybody could tan you up if you needed to be.

I was working for the Cartledge family, which is where my mother worked when she was alive. So after she died, they let me keep working for them. When I'd do my chores, I got a chance to go to school. Anyway, that's kind of how it started. My dad found out where I was when I was about 14. I lived alone until then.

My dad worked for a gentleman named Jim O'Reilly, an Irishman. He and my dad were very good friends. This may be funny to hear. But even then, with Jim Crow, segregation and all that, there were blacks and whites that were friends. And I thank God for it, because had it not been for some of the good white folks there wouldn't have been any black folks left because white people could kill you. They could do anything they wanted and nothing was ever done about it. So it was good to have a white friend.

A lot of the white people, I think, felt the same way about blacks because they could trust them. And when you could trust each other, it was really wonderful. Anyhow, my dad loved this guy so much, when I was born they named me Riley. My dad's last name was King. So when I got big enough to know what it meant, I asked him: "You named me after Mr. O'Reilly. What happened to the O?"

He said, "You didn't look Irish enough."

I was aware of differences in races very early. I was taught to say, "Mr. So-and-so" and "Mrs. So-and-so" to the white people. I wasn't taught that about the blacks, with exceptions. I later was taught that you give honor to whom honor is due.

My great-grandmother was a slave. She told me this story: In Houston, Mississippi, there was this boy who was going with the boss' daughter. It was in an area where if a black man was caught with a white woman, generally they called it rape. But this lady was different. Some people caught them together. Her dad was a big farmer, so the people in the area were going to lynch him. They had him chained to a pump, the iron part that sticks out of the ground. They had put tar and feathers on him, and they started to burn him while he was alive. And this lady, being the lady she was, told her father that she wasn't raped. She liked him. They liked each other. So she said to her father, in so many words, "Shoot him, don't let them punish him like that." So he did. He shot him. But they still burned him. But at least he didn't have to feel it.

I never saw a lynching, but saw a man's body shortly after it had happened. I remember one day coming from school, they had lynched a young man. And they had castrated him. They had brought him and laid him down near the entrance to the courthouse after dragging him through the city. That's when I had a chance to see him.

I don't really know how I felt. I just knew it could happen to me. It was like when I went in the army and they taught us if a bullet fell on your buddy, you'd be sad and hurt—but then you'd be glad it wasn't you.

The only advice I got then was, if you wanted to stay alive you must do certain things. If there were "colored" and "white" drinking fountains, drink out of the one that said "colored," because if you didn't you'd be in trouble.

The only bad thing I was ever taught was: Never fight with white people, but if you had to fight them, kill them, because they were

BLUESMAN B. B. KING picks a lick on his beloved guitar, Lucille, backstage in 1969. "Many times I've felt like I was being black twice," he says. "I got put down by white people because of my color and by my own people because I'm a blues singer."

going to kill you. There was hardly no in between. You either had to let go or be ready to die.

This is going to sound funny to you. I've had three white men who've been my mentors. One of them was the man that I worked for when my mother died, Mr. Cartledge. I was crazy about him. I thought he was a fair man. Fair to us means so much. It means that you may be white, you may be black or Chinese or Native American, whatever, but this man, if he thought a dime was yours, he'd give it to you. That's the kind of man he was.

Before I went to Memphis I worked for a man on the plantation named Johnson Barrett. Mr. Barrett, to me, was another one of those kind of people. When I worked for Mr. Barrett, he was sort of like a father. He didn't take no nonsense. But when I was doing what I was supposed to do, somehow he knew it. I didn't know it at the time, but many years later I learned that he was Jewish. To me, he was a great man. I wanted to be like him.

When I went to Memphis to try to be a musician, I met this gentleman named Burt Ferguson. He had the radio station there in Memphis. [WDIA, the first radio station in the South to feature black disc jockeys—including King—broadcast specifically to black listeners; it was here that King was nicknamed Beale Street Blues Boy, ultimately shortened to B. B.] I worked for him for quite a while, and I learned to love him, too.

I've got 26 people working for me now. I want to be like each one of these men I've mentioned. I want to be fair, treat them nicely. That's the way they did me.

You know, the old ideas are dying out. When there was segregation, young people weren't allowed to do certain things. Now that we're free, they do a lot of detrimental things, and that bothers me.

I have a son that just got 20 years in prison, and I'm sad about it. I talked with him and talked with him about the drugs. He wasn't selling them. He was using them. He got so hooked that once he didn't have any money he would do bad things, break in people's houses. At least that's what he was convicted of.

I guess in some way I'm glad that he was caught before he could hurt someone else, or got hurt himself. But that still makes me very sad, very sad—whether it's my son, your son, my daughter, your daughter, whomever. So many good young lives have been lost.

They claim a man is not supposed to cry. That's what I was brought up thinking. But I guess I destroy the thought of that, because I cry a lot, wondering why? Not just my son, but your son, his son, her son. Why can't they listen? Why can't they pay attention? Why do they have to destroy themselves? Maybe to them they're not destroying themselves, but to me they are.

My older cousin was a blues guitarist—Bukka White. One of the things he taught me was: If you want to be a blues singer, dress like you're going to the bank to borrow money. The reason for that is that we were always being put down. Many times I've felt like I was being black twice: I got put down by white people because of my color and by my own people because I'm a blues singer. (Even though I'm a blues singer, my mentors in music were jazz musicians like Duke Ellington, Count Basie, Benny Goodman, Woody Herman, Jimmy Lunceford.)

I wore overalls so long when I was on the plantation, I don't wear jeans anymore. To me, jeans are overalls with the bib cut off. I got a pair at home, but I never wear them in the streets. Never.

I don't really try to be sophisticated—that's not my idea. My idea is just to be respectful of what I do. I try to show people there's a different side to the myth that a blues singer is a guy that sits looking north with a cigarette hanging on the east side of his lip, a jug of corn liquor on his west side, and his pants torn on the south side.

*Clarence Gields was born in Buxtom, Ontario, in 1917, the grandson of slaves who had escaped to Canada via the Underground Railroad. His parents moved to Detroit when he was 5, and he grew up there, learning only when he went to enlist during World War II that he was not an American citizen. After serving 40 days in jail for being an "illegal alien," Gields decided not to enlist.*

*Still wiry, Gields suffers from asthma and arthritis, and has some bitter memories of life in the country his grandparents fled. One of his jobs during the 1940s and 1950s was selling and delivering building materials.*

I carried eight or ten tons of building material. And this day, there is a vacant lot, there's no address. East of this, north of this. That's how you find it.

A child—about four years old, I would say, not yet going to school—comes up to me and says, "Nigger." Just like that. I ignored it.

So he said it again: "Nigger." And he got good with it: "Nigger, nigger, nigger."

Every time he said that word, I wanted to knock the hell out of him. That's the way I felt. And this was in Dearborn, Michigan. No way would I have hit that boy, but that's the way I felt.

His father and mother had taught him a dirty word, was what I figured, so I decided to teach him something else to take back to them. Every doggone dirty word I knew, I tried to give to him.

I felt better after that. It relieved the pressure.

CHAPTER 4

# TWISTED STEEL AND SEX APPEAL

*Sputnik Monroe was a bad-guy wrestler who loved to be booed. He advertised himself as "235 pounds of twisted steel and sex appeal, with a body women love and men fear, rough, tough, and hard to bluff."*

*How bad was he? Listen to the Kansas-born Monroe describe his fighting style: "Win if you can, lose if you must, always cheat—and if they take you out, leave tearing down the ring."*

*A big mean white guy in a leotard makes an unlikely civil rights hero, but Monroe, 75, is that and much more. In his suburban Texas home, the chain-smoking Monroe recalled the night he picked a grudge match against racism in Memphis—and won.*

MY MOTHER'S FATHER WAS A bare-fist fighter. He got me started with the punching bag. He lived in a little town—Watonga, Oklahoma. I'd go down there in the summertime, and he'd buy an ice-cream cone for anybody who'd box me a round or two.

I started wrestling in ninth grade. My coach, Stub Mayo, said I didn't have a lot of finesse, but I might kill somebody with my aggressiveness. When I was 20 years old, I started wrestling with a carnival, taking on all comers. My name was Pretty Boy Rocque. The promoter in Louisville, Kentucky, thought I looked like Elvis, so they called me Elvis Roc Monroe. When you say "Roc Monroe" real fast, it sounds like "rock 'n' roll."

I was what's called a "heel" in professional wrestling, and I was the world's greatest. I'd wink at pretty girls and wave my hand and make the guy sitting next to her hot. Once, I was struttin' with my bag and this woman stopped in front of me; she told me I was an arrogant son-of-a-bitch and slapped me. I dropped the bag, did a pose for her and said, "How does it feel to touch a real man?"

Mobile, Alabama, was the beginning of my razoo [relationship] with the blacks. I had driven from Seattle to Greenville, Mississippi, and I pooped out. I was drinking coffee but falling asleep every five or 10 miles. In Greenville, there was a little black guy hitchhiking. I asked him if he could drive. He said, "Yes, sir."

I said, "All right, we're going to the television station in Mobile, Alabama. If you speed or anything I'm going break both your legs, 'cause I'm going to take a little nap."

He cruised all the way to the television station. When we got there, he carried my bag and I put my arm around him. An old lady saw that and called me a "nigger-lovin' motherfucker."

The insult just inspired me. When I went on TV, the curtain opened and I still had my arm around the little black guy. That set off the lady who had cussed me out. The security guard told her if she kept cursing, she was going to have to leave.

She said, "Well, that son-of-a-bitch is a goddamn Sputnik!"

I threw up my hands. The Russian *Sputnik* satellite had gone up three days before, but I didn't know anything about it. But everybody else—the ring announcer, the commentator—everybody picked up on it.

That was a Saturday night. Monday when I went to work, I did a radio interview. The announcer asked, "Well, Sputnik, what do you think of the South?" The name "Sputnik" angered a lot of people [because the Russians were first in space]. That started it.

The promoter in Mobile took me to Memphis and surrounding towns. They'd never had the kind of attendance that I produced for them. The blond streak in my hair and my loud mouth brought in the crowds. I'd say things to obnoxious fans like, "Sit down, ignorant, everybody knows you're here."

Blacks loved me because the whites hated me. I was called "the general of the little nigger army." I think my black fans passed the word around from Mobile to Memphis. I embraced them. I hung out on Beale Street in pool halls and theaters and at Lansky Brothers, the place where Elvis bought his clothes. This was 1958.

On the Saturday morning wrestling show on television, the studio had room for 10 blacks. At Ellis Auditorium, where we wrestled, there were about 90 seats in the high, high balcony where blacks could sit. That was it.

I told the manager of the Ellis Auditorium, "If you don't let my colored friends in, I'm leaving."

You would have thought I had declared independence when I told them that. They knew I wasn't a bullshitter. If I told you I was leaving, I'm leaving.

The mayor told me I shouldn't be creating racial differences. I said, "There's not any racial differences—they're black and I'm white, and we both know it." I told him if he said anything else to me about it, I'd knock him on his ass.

But the promoters didn't want the loss at the box office, so they said, "Yes, sir." That's all they could say to me.

The stage in the Ellis Auditorium was in the middle of the building. The south side was elevated for bands, with a band pit. So they opened the curtains and put 2,000 more people in there—all of them black. For about a month there would be a couple of thousand standing outside waiting to get in. They were sold out.

I had a lot of fights on the street: "Take a swing at me," I'd say. "Call me a nigger-lovin' son-of-a-bitch." I was tougher than anybody they had in Memphis, Tennessee.

Once I was with two black wrestlers and we stopped to eat in some little town in Mississippi. They went in the back door, and I went with them. Damn near caused a riot. All the white people got hot.

I went back two years ago and got hugged and kissed on Beale Street. People told me they loved me for what I did for them. It brings tears to my eyes when they hug me and tell me they love me and that I was the greatest. They'd never seen me wrestle, but their parents or grandparents or somebody told them about me. I made a big difference in their city. And we should have done that in a lot of cities.

The Man Upstairs must have had something to do with this. I'm not a psychiatrist. I don't try to figure people out. If I can't figure them out, I kick their ass.

CHAPTER 5

# GENTLEMAN OF THE PRESS

*In a career spanning 57 years, Vernon Jarrett has won nearly every major journalism award. At the dawn of the Civil Rights Movement, he stood at the vanguard of journalists who wrote about the black experience. Jarrett devoted his professional life to writing for* The Chicago Defender, *the largest black-owned daily newspaper in America. And he made it his goal in every article to expose injustice.*

MY GRANDFATHER WAS A TEENage runaway slave in the Civil War, but he was so illiterate he didn't know where he was from. He used to make my brother read *The Chicago Defender* out loud from cover to cover. I was too young to read, so I just sat back and enjoyed it. We didn't know until after he died that my grandfather couldn't read.

My grandmother learned how to read by stealing it. She used to sit outside the home of this white family while they were being tutored. They had chalkboards, but outside the house she wrote in the dirt.

To me, journalism is a vehicle for taking a stand and doing the most good for our race. When I moved to Chicago and started working for the *Defender* in 1946, my first story was covering a race riot at the Airport Homes project, where a mob tried to kill some black veterans.

Chicago had a legal provision called "restrictive covenants"—clauses inserted in housing contracts and deeds and signed by a majority of the members of a community—that committed them not to sell, rent, or lease said property to people of the Negro race (or, in some instances, to Orientals or Jews). The covenants were mostly directed at blacks, and because the community had made them contractual, they became legally binding.

Black people were therefore restricted to little pockets of the city, jammed on top of each other. Chicago was about to explode. Black people were moving out because they just could not take the torment. Panic usually struck when the first black moved into a nonrestricted block that was all white, or any community that was all white. The word would go out—"The niggers are coming!"—and a mob would gather in front of your apartment or your house.

Airport Homes was a collection of duplexes on the South Side that had been thrown up during World War II. It covered several blocks. The property had been turned over to the Chicago Housing Authority (CHA) because it was government-owned property. Rather than restricting access, the CHA director established a rule of first come, first served for war veterans, regardless of creed or color.

One black veteran—he'd had some ribs shot away in Italy—was about to move into Airport Homes, and I was out there the evening he turned in his lease. A mob gathered and chased the veterans and the journalists, white and black, up into the second floor of a duplex.

They had their little kids with them and they was chanting, "Niggers go home! Niggers go home!" They tried to set fire to the building. One black veteran got on the phone and called the police station. He said, "You got some cops standing around out here chatting with these people. They're trying to kill us, and it's getting dark!"

The veteran on the phone told the cops, "I'm going to my car to get my switchblade. If you don't have these cops give me some protection, somebody's going to get hurt." That's when the cops standing there with the mob came up and led us through. They escorted us to our cars because they thought that veteran would really kill someone.

When we got in the car, I heard all the crap I used to tolerate growing up in Paris, Tennessee: "You niggers think you can come out here and get our white women!" In the South, nobody ever spit on me, but at Airport Homes, they did. Some white women were part of our group as observers; they had thought it would be a nice little thing. The mob was hysterical over that. They were shouting at those white girls: "Which one of these niggers you going to fuck tonight?"

Some of the crowd tried to turn over the car I was in. They bashed in the windows with a baseball bat. This was December, and it was cold. But it was a funny thing—all of us brothers who were out there, we were ready to fight. The black veteran whose story I was covering had been in Italy so long he spoke conversational Italian. He came out of the car, ripped open his shirt, and pointed to his scars: "This happened in Anzio!" Then he said it in Italian. And then he started crying.

The crowd just stood there startled. Some of the older guys felt guilty. The younger white veterans were there because their veterans' organization had demanded that the project be turned over to veterans. They hadn't anticipated black veterans moving in.

I jumped out of the car and stood up there with him. This little white boy, an ex-soldier, came up to both of us, trembling. "I know what all of you guys want. I was in England. I saw you with those white girls." I said to him, "You didn't see me in no goddamn England—I was in Hawaii!" Then a big cop came up and separated us.

One of their leaders looked like a pretty nice guy. He was Italian, but when this black soldier started talking in Italian, I don't think the guy understood it. Louis Jourdan, the musician, wrote this song called "Caledonia" that went, "Caldonia! Caldonia! What makes your big head so hard?" On my next trip out to Airport Homes, the Italian guy was leading the crowd in a chant: "Caldonia! Caldonia! If you stay tonight, we gonna have fried nigger babies in the morning!"

It was my first glimpse of what shape America was in, in terms of race. It made you real mean, man. I haven't lost some of that yet.

The white newspapers had an agreement with the Mayor's Commission on Human Relations: They would treat this story as though it never happened. They were trying to avoid a repeat of Red Summer [in Chicago, 13 days of racial clashes starting on July 27, 1919, that killed 15 whites and 23 blacks]. The *Defender* was the only one that ran the story. The editors suggested our bylines not appear on most of the stories, but I didn't give a damn—I was trying to change the world.

*One of the first major civil rights battles happened in World War II, when black men joined the military in droves and encountered harsh racial bias. One gung-ho fighting man—David Dinkins, still 47 years away from becoming New York City's first black mayor—had to move a mountain of prejudice just to join the Marines.*

"The way to survive the war is to be well trained," I thought as I watched newsreels of troops storming the beaches. "And the way to be well trained is to be a Marine."

There was no recruiting office in Trenton, New Jersey, so I went to Jersey City, then Newark, New York, Camden, and Philadelphia. At each place I was told, "You have to go to the state of your residence" or, "We have our quota of Negro Marines."

I was real little and naturally I thought I was bad because I'm small. Eventually, a recruiting officer in Philadelphia agreed to accept me. He wrote a letter to my draft board: "If this man passes the physical, put him in the Marine Corps." That's how persistent I had been.

Jim Crow hit home in a graphic way. White recruits were trained at Parris Island, South Carolina, while blacks were trained at Camp Lejeune, North Carolina. When I went south I stepped off the train and was about to get on a bus when I was told, "You go 'round back." I had to go to the "Colored" window to get my ticket.

It was all so illogical. Here we're going to fight this war to end all wars, yet we got second-class citizenship. As far as I knew, there weren't going to be white bullets and black bullets. There weren't going to be white graves and black graves. We were all going to be together—or so I thought. But when those Marines who may have thought Jim Crow was okay got pinned down under fire in places like Guam, boy—they just loved to see black Marines landing and bringing ammo. They were so relieved and delighted they hugged them.

CHAPTER 6

# SKIN DIVE

*Sammy Lee always thought of himself as an all-American boy. His parents had been born in Korea, but as he grew up in Fresno, California, Lee dreamed of representing the United States as an Olympic diver.*

*That dream came true in London in 1948, when Lee became the first Asian American to win an Olympic gold medal. Four years later he won again, making him the first male diver to win back-to-back golds.*

*Now a retired physician in Southern California, Lee, 83, recalled how he overcame wartime racism to make his childhood passion come true—thanks to the punishing guidance of a coach who was himself a relentless racist. That life-changing experience opened his eyes to his own private prejudices.*

THEY SAY THERE ARE NO ATHEISTS on the starting line or at the Olympics. I prayed to God, and in case he wasn't listening, to Allah, Mohammed, and Buddha. The pool had a skylight, and when I went up to do my last dive—a forward three-and-a-half somersault—the sun broke through the clouds and I thought, "Oh, Jesus Christ." I knew I was going to win.

As I hit the water, I thought I'd done a belly flop. Everything was tingling. And when I broke the surface, I was in pain. I looked up and saw my score—9.5, 10. The pain stopped. When I walked out of that pool it was the second time in history that man walked on water.

My dream of becoming an Olympic champion was born during

the 1932 Games in Los Angeles, when I noticed the flags of the participating countries in a tunnel leading to downtown Los Angeles.

"What are those flags?" I asked my father.

"They're having the Olympic Games," he said. "That's where they crown the greatest athletes in the world."

Then and there, I got Olympic fever: "Papa, some day I'm going to be an Olympic champ." A chill went up and down my spine.

That summer I was swimming at Brookside Pool on the one day a week when nonwhites were admitted. We were playing follow-the-leader, and I was leading the pack and diving. My best friend, an African American kid named Hart Crum, challenged me: "Hey, Sammy, why do you only do one somersault?"

"Because I don't know how to do anything else," I said.

"Well, I'll bounce the board," said Hart, "and when I yell, you come out into a dive."

He taught me how to do a forward one-and-a-half somersault. I was thrilled. I ran home. "Papa," I said, "I found my sport. I'm going to be an Olympic champ in diving."

My parents owned a little chop suey restaurant. I would throw anybody out of the restaurant who said to my father, "Hey, Charlie." I'd say, "His name's not Charlie—that's Mr. Lee."

My dad said, "We have to take this stuff in order to make a living. You stay in the back where you can't hear. Study hard to become a doctor. Become a diving champion. Don't listen to all this other stuff."

I was working as a pool boy (along with pool girl Esther Williams) at the L. A. Swim Stadium. One day I'm swimming and I see this great big guy who looks like the Jolly Green Giant on the other side of the 50-meter pool. He's smoking a cigarette.

I walk over and he says, "Hey, kid. You like to dive?"

"I love it," I answer.

"Lemme see you do a swan dive."

So I did, and I felt pretty good about it. I come out and he says, "Who taught you that dive?"

"That kid over there." I point to Hart Crum.

"Go kick him in the ass," he says. "That was the worst goddamn dive I ever saw."

Jesus, I thought. Who the hell is this guy? After a couple more

OLYMPIC CHAMPION Sammy Lee streaks toward a gold medal in diving at the 1948 Olympics in Wembley, England. The son of Korean immigrants, Lee battled racial prejudice from his own coach. He won a second Olympic medal in 1952.

dives, he goes up to Olympic swimming champion Duke Paoa Kahanamoku and I hear him say, "See that Chink down there? I'm going to make him the world's greatest diver, or kill him."

I walk up to the guy and say, "Sir, I'm no Chink. I'm a Korean."

He turns me around and gives me a kick in the butt. "I don't give a goddamn if you're a Filipino. Get up there on that diving board."

Up on the board, I say to a friend, "After this dive I'm going to hit that big son-of-a-bitch in the mouth and run like hell."

My friend says, "If you ever swallowed your pride, now's the time. That guy is the answer to your prayers. He's Jim Ryan; he knows diving."

I swallowed my pride, but I said to myself, "Just this one time."

A few months later I met this Egyptian guy, Farid Simaika, who Ryan had coached to a silver medal in 1928. Simaika said, "Sam, you know why he's so hard on you? Because you'll be the first nonwhite Olympic diving champion—but not unless you are 30 to 40 points better than the white man. That's why he's so tough on you."

Ryan sure was racist. If we went to a restaurant that served blacks, he would get up and leave. He'd say to me, "Tell them to go to hell." During my comeback for the 1952 Olympics, he yelled out to me, "Hey, you dumb Chink! You're not supposed to dive like that!"

"Jim," I said, "you know I'm a professional now. How can people respect me if you talk to me like that?"

He said, "If you don't like it, you son-of-a-bitch, the hell with you." And he walked out.

Ryan was an enigma. During the 1952 Olympics, even though he was no longer my coach, he came to my mother's place, worried about whether I was going to win. He attended my wedding in 1950. He respected my family, yet he was a bigot.

After Pearl Harbor we used to wear a big button with a Korean flag, an American flag, and the words "I'm a Korean, not a Jap." I was wearing that button on my way to the national swim championships in 1942. I happened to go on a troop train, and I bumped into a couple of Japanese Americans on the Hawaiian swim team.

"Hey, Sam," they said. "How are you?"

I had this button on, and I said, "I'm really embarrassed."

They said, "Ah, Sam. We understand. Don't worry about it."

I took that button off and never wore it again.

CHAPTER 7

# AMERICAN GANDHI

*Returning from a visit to India more than 50 years ago, the Rev. James Lawson took Mahatma Gandhi's teachings of passive resistance and combined them with his black Christian upbringing to create a philosophy of nonviolence that revolutionized the American Civil Rights Movement.*

*Lawson's father was a Canadian-born African Methodist Episcopal (AME) Zion pastor, the grandson of a slave who had escaped to the North. His mother came to the United States from Jamaica as a nanny at age 18. Together they shaped the outlook that infused in him a burning desire to seek a just society for all people.*

*At 76, Lawson—silver haired and straight backed—still has the barrel-chested build of a fullback. Sitting in his office at the Los Angeles branch of the Southern Christian Leadership Conference, Lawson recalled one of his earliest encounters with prejudice—and the reaction to it that surprised even him.*

FOR WHATEVER REASON, FROM early on I knew I was somebody. At age 10 or 11—fourth or fifth grade—I was running down Main Street on an errand for my mother. It was a warm, beautiful spring day, car windows were wide open, and a young child stuck his head out the car window as I passed by and yelled at me. "Nigger!"

I walked over to the car and I smacked the child.

Where that came from, I still don't know. I have to tell you this: It came from somewhere deep inside me.

Back at home I told my mother what occurred. She turned to face me—she was working at the stove—and quietly said something I'll never forget: "Jimmy, what good did that do?"

When she asked that, she reinforced a lot of things the family believed in—faith in Jesus and the church and that sort of thing.

Her next sentence I also remember very clearly: "There must be a better way."

It was a sanctification—a conversion of spirit for me at that early age. I heard something very deep inside me saying, "You will never again use your fists in anger. You will never again strike back in that fashion when you get insulted in some way."

From that moment, I was conscientiously launched on a journey of discovering a better way—which, I came to realize, was the way of the love of Jesus. Later on, at college and in divinity school, I saw that when Jesus said, "If someone hits you on the left cheek, turn to him the other cheek," it was a form of resistance. It was a call to find a better way to fight back.

Around age 18, in 1947, I began to read Gandhi's autobiography. I realized that what Gandhi was doing and saying had been happening to me on a personal level. Acquiescence or passivity basically means you run away from oppression or you live under it.

Slaves in the United States who ran away from slavery were not fleeing—they were moving toward liberation. But in the case of acquiescence or passivity, that form of flight is yielding to the oppression and letting it take management of your own soul, your own life.

That's what too many people in oppressive systems do: They internalize it and become passive. They may become quite angry in their own family or in their own neighborhood. They may even escape into alcohol as the only way to live with themselves. But all of that is part of the same pattern. It does not get redirected to resisting stuff that has you in stress, in pain. It doesn't chip away at that.

Finding ways to resist inwardly and outwardly, as I sometimes put it now, is the quest at the very heart of nonviolent struggle. I know people who lived in slavery, but who maintained the integrity of their own lives within it. That's a form of resistance.

In 1951, I went on trial for refusing to report for induction into the military. I was sentenced to three years in prison, and ended up at a maximum-security facility in Ashland City, Kentucky.

I was frightened. I was threatened with gang rape. One night, I was so terrified I paced the floor of my cell, swinging a lightweight steel chair that I planned to use as a weapon. Then, somewhere in the early morning, I heard a voice: "Jim? What is this? What's going on? Why are you afraid? You are not here by your own choice. I sent you here."

The fear seemed to drain out of my system. I felt enormous confidence and peace. And I knelt at that chair by the cell window, prayed, and asked forgiveness.

Early on I had met a man named Liberty. He was a mugger from Washington, D.C.—a weight trainer who had spent half his life in jail—but I treated him with dignity and respect. We became friends, and I think he told everyone in the cell house to leave me alone.

After I was paroled in 1952, I went to India as a missionary for the United Methodist Church. My three years there were an awakening. I lived in a Hindu culture, wore Hindu garb, and grew as a human being. Most important, I came face-to-face with America's Cold War policies. I had to stand up and say, "My country is wrong. I am a critic of that policy."

Back in the U.S., as I got involved in the Civil Rights Movement in the '60s, I tried to teach that when we went to jail, we should turn the jail into a classroom. We might not have books—though oftentimes we did—but we had conversations on the struggle, conversations on nonviolence, conversations on our own ambitions, aspirations, and spiritual discipline. We tried to turn prison into a way station for discovering more about ourselves and more about our struggle.

From 1959 and 1960 in the movement, demonstrators would carry a book in their back pocket, because if they were arrested they were going to need that book. If they didn't have a book, they tried to talk to the other prisoners.

Sometimes, under the direct orders of white guards and white sheriffs who said, "Do this or else," these prisoners turned cruel. My friends Fannie Lou Hamer and Annelle Ponder were beaten and seriously injured for the rest of their lives; part of the beating came from fellow black prisoners using blackjacks under the eyes of the sheriffs.

VISIONARY LEADER Mohandas Gandhi reads in 1946 by his spinning wheel, a symbol of India's struggle for independence. Gandhi's philosophy of nonviolence became a moral beacon for the Rev. James Lawson and other civil rights activists.

In Birmingham, Alabama, in 1963, [Public Safety Commissioner] Bull Connor had no conscience about turning high-powered water hoses on children and women, knocking them down in the streets. Remember that we had no conscience whatsoever about decades of the lynching of mostly black people in horrible ways. We had no conscience about executing black people and poor people for crimes for which a white person is not executed.

This comes hauntingly out of the past. I mean, it's not something that we've invented. It comes out of this dreadful past that we have tended to deny and that we refuse to face—a hidden wound in the very soul of America.

Part of the reason we have such shameless leadership today is because of the assassinations of the 1960s. I'm convinced of that. Those assassinations changed our country forever. The four most notable assassinations were of young men in their 30s and 40s who were emerging with a voice calling the nation to a different way of thinking about itself. The killers wiped out the men who were moving the country in a different direction.

It made it possible for Richard Nixon to be elected. Had our leadership remained on the course of a dream for the country that embraced everybody, Nixon never would have been elected. Most of the presidents we've had since then would not have made it.

Martin Luther King would have been the moral voice of the nation, as he was already in the '60s. He probably would not have endorsed anyone, but he would have been teaching and preaching and writing in such a fashion that many people would have had a different moral compass.

King said we have difficult days ahead of us. Given where the nation is today, with the politics and economics of the nation making for plantation capitalism, it's very likely we will become increasingly authoritarian. But there's hope. Yes, I think there is real hope.

*Black filmmaker St. Clair Bourne recounts a scene from early 1963 when, as a 19-year-old ROTC cadet lieutenant majoring in international relations at Georgetown University, he and some friends went out late one chilly night to get something to eat.*

The thing about this whole event for me was that I went through it like an out-of-body experience. I was in the middle of it, but I was very conscious about what was happening. It was as if I were making a film of it.

To get food late at night you had to drive across Key Bridge to Arlington, Virginia. So at about 12:30 in the morning some friends and I jumped in a car and went to a luncheonette. I noticed that when we walked in, people kind of looked at me, but I didn't think that much about it. I just sat down and had the audacity to ask for a strawberry milk shake and a hamburger.

The guy said, "We don't serve your kind here."

I looked at him, and I didn't really understand what he meant. But then I did understand it, and I got up, undecided about what I was going to do. The rest of the guys got up and went outside, so I went out with them. We were talking about it on the drive back when I suddenly said, "Wait a minute—he can't do that to me! I'm going back."

The next day I called the Nonviolent Action Group at Howard University and asked Stokely Carmichael, the head of the organization, what to do. He gave me some tips about going in: "Don't start yelling. Be polite. Let them make the first move." Things like that.

That night, a bunch of white guys showed up at my dorm room door and said, "We're going back there with you." They were all from a fraternity of Foreign Service School students, and there were about a dozen of them.

You know how when you see pictures of sit-ins now, you always see the black cook looking through the window of the kitchen door? Well, that's actually what happened when we walked in. The cook looked at me and smiled. I smiled back, but you could tell he couldn't say a word.

When I refused to leave the restaurant, they called the cops. The cops were rough, but they didn't beat us up. Remember now, I was the only black person and these other kids were from Georgetown. The cops knew these were not just working-class kids—they were the sons of rich people—so the cops couldn't do anything to them. They arrested us and I went to jail, but I got out the same night. After that I stopped going to class. I opted out.

All this political consciousness had me in shock. I was reeling. I was represented in Arlington County court by a black civil rights lawyer named Frank Reeves. Someone else represented all the white kids. The case kept being postponed because they didn't really want to convict the white kids.

If I had to do it over, I would do the same thing. Back then I was just stumbling—basically reeling from one scene to another. But I knew that what I was doing was right. I also knew I could not continue to live the way I had been, which was learning how, as a future member of the U.S. Foreign Service, to represent a country that treated me like a second-class citizen.

CHAPTER 8

# THE BIRTH OF ELVIS

*To passersby on the two-lane blacktop winding through the Hill Country of northern Mississippi, the eclectic collection on the other side of the gate—a weather-beaten barn, a one-room frame house, an old school bus—might be nothing more than a duct-taped testament to Southern poverty. But Memphis musician and record producer Jim Dickinson deems it the lap of luxury. The barn doubles as his recording studio.*

*"You have everything a man could want," Bob Dylan told him when he visited the spread. "A man could do a lot of thinking here."*

*Dickinson makes a passionate case for Memphis being the greatest music city in modern history. The home of Elvis Presley was for all practical purposes the birthplace of rock 'n' roll. It is also the place where blues, rhythm 'n' blues, and soul, hillbilly, rockabilly, and country & western were mixed and blended. To achieve this feat in the 1940s and '50s, Memphis musicians such as Dickinson, both black and white, defied Jim Crow laws and crossed color lines to make music.*

WHEN WE DROVE INTO THE driveway of our new home in Memphis, the first thing I saw was Alec. His name was Timothy Teal, but they called him Alec because he was a smart alec. He was real short. He became my teacher.

He took it upon himself as part of his job as our yardman to teach me the things I needed to know, and not be a wise-ass Yankee kid, which I was. He taught me how to throw a knife underhanded, how to shoot craps, how to play card games like pittypat and smut. He was a great singer but he didn't play an instrument. When he learned I wanted to play music, he brought me musicians to teach me. It was very Uncle Remus. I know that's politically incorrect, but that's what it was. It was also probably the most valuable relationship of my life outside my family.

Alec must have been in his late twenties. He was very much the young buck. They called him The Ram in the neighborhood. He stabbed a couple guys. My father had to get him out of jail periodically. He was an inspirational role model for a boy.

We referred to the black section of town as being "down the road." It was like another world, and totally inaccessible. Old man Orr, who owned the grocery at Orr's Corner, would lend blacks money at real high interest rates, a real plantation mentality. My father, who worked for the Diamond Match Company, was the anti-Mr. Orr, in that he employed several people who hung out at Orr's Corner and lent them money. He was very much the captain, and was treated that way, so in that sense I grew up with a double standard.

The most motivating thing that happened to me during that period of time was seeing the Memphis Jug Band—Will Shade, Charlie Burse, Good Kid—the most important jug band of all time, with roots dating back to the 1920s. I saw them downtown with my father one Saturday afternoon. It was so transcultural. Will Shade singing, "Come on down to my house, Honey. There's nobody home but me," and playing this zinc-tub bass, while Good Kid played a washboard with drumsticks. To a nine-year-old white kid, it was like hearing Martians play music.

It utterly changed my life.

After hearing that band, other things in life just didn't seem to be as important. I spent the next 10, 15 years of my life trying to find that music. It was right down the road, literally, but I couldn't get there in 1950. A white kid couldn't go where the music was.

Several years later, Alec brought me a piano player to teach me. They called him Dishrag and he was legendary in Memphis. He was dead drunk the day I saw him. He never even took his overcoat or hat off. He just sat down at my mother's piano, and started to play like nothing I'd ever heard.

I asked him if he knew, "Come On Down to My House, Honey, There's Nobody Home But Me." He grinned and said, "How do you know that song? That song's older than you are."

He told me everything in music was made up of "codes." I thought he meant codes like secret codes, Captain Marvel, Morse Code. Of course, he meant chords, but I heard "codes," and thought to myself, "No wonder I can't damn well do it. My mother didn't tell me it was code. This guy's about to give me the secret here."

And he did.

With that piece of information from him, with a chord in my right hand and an octave in my left hand, that's all I needed to play rock 'n' roll. To this day, that's basically what I do. I play an octave and a major triad. If you play it back and forth between your hands, right, left, right, left, then you have a shuffle. If you play it straight, you've got eighth-note rock 'n' roll.

That's the racial difference.

The crux is how the implied eighth-notes of rock 'n' roll are handled. Whether it's politically incorrect or not, I don't care. It's absolutely true. Black people do it one way. White people do it another way. The difference is feeling, therefore interior. Not to be too anthropologic.

After I'd been to college and supposedly knew better, I signed my first record deal with Ruben Cherry's Home of the Blues label. Ruben had a record store on Beale Street. Of course, he was a white Jewish guy. Everybody on the label but me was black. He would play my tape for a roomful of people and have them guess who was singing. They'd guess everybody who was black before they picked me. He called me Little Muddy.

Ruben used to take me to these various black functions where we'd be the only white people. One night I came home drunk. A picture of me with Ike and Tina Turner fell out of my sport coat pocket when my mother hung it up the next morning. There was hell to pay. My father said, "Don't you realize this would ruin my business?" And it would've, then. My parents, who were good Christian people, didn't think of themselves as racists, but they were.

The older I got, the worse it got. But the music was always the problem. The only time I heard my parents speak the N-word was in

ROCK 'N' ROLL ICON Elvis Presley shakes up a crowd of fans in 1957. Elvis's sound, a mix of black and white musical influences, broke racial barriers and ushered in a new era of freedom.

regards to the music, not any human being or person: "Why do you have to play that loud nigger music?"

I'll tell you why. Because it was in my head and it was driving me crazy.

One of the most important things Alec showed me was WDIA [the Memphis radio station that was the first in America to be programmed by African Americans for African Americans]. This was not common knowledge in the white community in 1950. Everything was segregated, even the damned radio.

That's what Dewey Phillips did that was so revolutionary. He's the disc jockey credited with playing Elvis Presley on the radio for the very first time. Which would have been enough, if that was all he ever did. But what Dewey really did was create the mindset that was Elvis Presley.

Elvis heard "That's All Right, Mama" on Dewey's "Red, Hot & Blue" radio show on WHBQ because he was the only white man who played black music. There were four radio stations that played white music for white people, and two black stations that played black music for black people. Dewey would come on the air and he'd play his theme music and say, "Ho, ho, good people," because that's who he was talking to—good people. He played good music for good people. He'd play Hank Williams and then he'd play gospel singer Sister Rosetta Tharpe. This created a mindset in Memphis that's still there.

Think about the 45's Elvis recorded for Sun Records. On one side of each record was a jump blues song—or "black" music—and on the other was a country ballad, "white" music. This is what was happening in Memphis at the time. The rural blacks coming to town and the rural whites coming to town—rednecks, if you will—were culturally colliding. And what was coming out was Elvis Presley.

It's freedom. It does the same thing to me that it does to everybody all over the world. It symbolizes individual freedom of expression. That's what it is.

To find it, it's like my first music lessons when I couldn't see the music. I would have never understood music in the European tradition. I still don't. But when I heard black music, something happened. And it wasn't just me. It was a whole generation of crazy white boys. That's what rock 'n' roll is: us trying to be them.

CHAPTER 9

# THE JUMP-OFF POINT

*Call it courage or ignorance, but from an early age Jerome Smith assumed he was entitled to every right enjoyed by Louisiana's white residents. His formal activism began when he was an 18-year-old sophomore at Southern University in Baton Rouge—but his first act of indignant defiance came long before that.*

WHEN I WAS NINE OR TEN—this would have been in the late 1940s—I got on a bus and took down the "Colored" screen and sat down in the white section. I had seen my father, a seaman, do something similar. When he did it, no one had reacted. But when I did it, the white people on the bus became very hostile. The conductor said he was going to slap me, that I had no business sitting by white folks.

An elderly black lady came from the back of the car. She slapped me on the head and said, "You should be ashamed of yourself, disturbing these good white folks." She pleaded with the people on the bus: "I'm gonna bring this little bad-behind boy back home; let me take care of him. I'm sorry this happened."

We got off the bus and went into a store. She hugged me and said, "Never stop doing what you're doing. Never stop taking that sign down." Then she cried, and said a prayer.

That was the jump-off point for me.

My mother was the well from which I drew much of my strength.

She worked as a domestic but also cultivated her natural talents—photographer, furniture maker, seamstress. She taught us all to stand up for our dignity.

We lived in a house where we had to catch the water in pots when it rained. White folks would come out to buy the dresses my mother sewed by hand. One time they wanted to buy a bedspread she had made and some curtains—very elaborate. The spread was her own design—similar to patchwork, with geometric patterns in fantastic shades of blue.

"I can't sell that," she told them. "That's for my children."

"Well, if you refuse to sell us this," they said, "we can't buy the other items."

My mother said, "Well, you won't buy them, then!"

That stuck with me. It meant that even though we lived in a little raggedy house, what we had in there were treasures—and that was something white folks could not get.

My mother used to say, "You're black, but you don't have to be dirty. You're black, but you don't have to be dumb. You're black, and the children of the people that I work for are not smarter than you. They cannot do the things you do." That is true. I could walk in their neighborhood, but they were afraid to walk in mine.

I was not taught to fear whites. I guess they did not have the same kind of social toughness. Part of their fear was based on guilt, knowing what their people had done to us.

*In 1961 Smith joined a Congress of Racial Equality–sponsored Freedom Ride from New Orleans to McComb, Mississippi, intent on desegregating the local Greyhound bus station.*

When we entered the McComb bus station, all these white folks came pouring into the station shouting, "Niggers!" and "Kill 'em!" They were beating us with brass knuckles and fists and sticks. I was being overwhelmed by some folks and my friend George Raymond intervened; he pretty much saved my life. He enabled me to remove myself from a danger zone while he absorbed the beating.

We made our way from the station into the streets, and just then an old man came through with a dirty old truck. He was the kind of person some might call an "Uncle Tom." In the back of the truck was stuff to feed his pigs. I was sort of unconscious, going in and out, but I remember him saying, "Can you see the truck?"

I must have answered, "Yeah."

He said, "Roll over into it."

He was the only person who could get through because he was like the white folks' "uncle." They didn't think he would do anything. He picked up me and another fellow, Thomas Valentine, hid us in the animal feed, and drove us to an old juke joint back into the woods outside McComb near "Nigger Town," as they used to call it. Burke Marshall [the assistant attorney general in charge of the Justice Department's Civil Rights Division] found out we was there. He called and said he wanted us to stop protesting. We were in pretty bad shape, so he said, "You need to go to the hospital."

I said, "You deal with this just like you would if President Kennedy was down here. We're not stopping. We're going back."

TOURING THE MISSISSIPPI DELTA near Greenville in April 1967, Senator Robert Kennedy *(right)* and activist Marian Wright Edelman hear from one woman what it's like to be poor in America. Newsman Daniel Schorr takes notes.

*Smith did go back, but he never discovered the name of the old man who had rescued him from the mob. Later he went to New York City to get medical treatment for the beatings. While there, he met with Marshall and Attorney General Robert Kennedy. Also present were James Baldwin, Dr. Kenneth Clark, Lena Horne, Harry Belafonte, and Lorraine Hansberry.*

Our people always put themselves up for struggle. Many of the unknown paid a tremendous price. It was all about our collective spiritual strength. The collective thing was much more powerful than Dr. King, much more powerful than whatever my humble contributions were.

I think of so many people who did so much. One of them was Lena Horne. She really was an unsung hero. In that meeting in New York, Robert Kennedy and I were having some words, and she went right at him. The Kennedys were part of her world, but she didn't allow them to trespass on what was sacred to her. She told Kennedy, point blank, "What you and your brother see as great steps in the struggle is not enough."

Another time, right after Medgar Evers was murdered, she was in Mississippi for an NAACP concert. She was very fair in terms of skin tone, but very black inside. She and Lorraine Hansberry contributed the station wagon that the three civil rights workers [James Chaney, Andrew Goodman, and Michael Schwerner] were murdered in. She took care of a lot of our basic needs. She made you feel that she belonged to us, and that whatever she was doing in terms of service was an honor. She didn't impose that star thing.

The things I think about when I look back are not the major events but the day-to-day dangers. To face those monsters every day with no cameras rolling, plain ordinary people had to extend their hand and help you get your job done.

All the fear was never in the moment itself. It was always after, when you'd think about what you'd done, what you'd been through, and tremble. Most times I would try to deal with the moment with a kind of emotional detachment you find in some of Gandhi's teaching, because you cannot surrender. You have to keep moving forward.

*White civil rights lawyer Charles Oldham was imparting the fundamentals of nonviolent dissent to CORE volunteers in St. Louis when he got some unwelcome opportunities to practice what he was teaching.*

One of our projects was to recruit blacks to this concept of nonviolence. We had a "CORE action discipline" where you had to commit yourself to nonviolence and agree to certain precepts before you could participate in a CORE project. We took it very seriously.

Anybody who came into the group had to go through this sort of philosophical discussion and training. We staged social dramas where people would be sitting-in and somebody else would come up and shove them or curse at them.

One time in the early 1960s we were at the Fordham Cafeteria and the harassment got real. People came in and started hitting us with rolled-up magazines. The police arrived and wanted us to swear out a warrant. We wouldn't do that—it would only have targeted us for more attacks—so nobody was arrested.

After the demonstration, Joe Ames, Marvin Rich, and I got on a streetcar, and three or four other white guys followed us on. We decided to get off, and the streetcar stop happened to be in a black neighborhood. Our attackers stayed on that streetcar.

Before we engaged in any demonstrations, we would go into the store or restaurant and meet with the owner or employees to present our side. We always dressed properly, and our negotiating teams never consisted of a white male and a black female, or a black male and a white female. That would have been too much of a distraction from what we were trying to do.

I was demonstrating inside a cafeteria when the owner, a big beefy guy about 6′2″, picked me up and just physically deposited me on the sidewalk. As soon as he went back in, I walked back inside and got right back in line again. For some reason, he didn't bother me after that.

CHAPTER 10

# "LIKE LITTLE TORTURES EACH DAY"

*In 1960 Carol Swann, then 12, was chosen—with one other student, Gloria Mead—to integrate the eighth grade of Chandler Junior High School in Richmond. Swann was lucky: There was no violent backlash. There was, however, a lot of resentment from other students, which she still remembers in vivid detail.*

MY PARENTS AND I NEVER considered not going, because we had made a commitment to the struggle. It was an obligation that you had to your people. It was a double-edged sword for me because if I did anything wrong, if I made any mistakes, I was letting myself down, my family down, the entire race.

Gloria and I had a meeting with the school administration before the start of school and were told that we should ignore anything that happened. "If people are teasing you, ignore it," they said. "They'll become tired of it and leave you alone."

The newspaper published our parents' names and addresses the June before we entered school. Almost immediately, we began to get threatening phone calls. My parents didn't curse. But in a week I think I heard every word there was, just by virtue of those phone calls. All summer. The callers hoped we would not go to school, and they could say to the courts, "Well, you know, we offered a spot to them and they declined—it's not our fault."

Gloria and I didn't know each other before this, but we grew to

BURDENED BY RACIAL EXPECTATIONS, Gloria Jean Mead and Carol Irene Swann (in a *Life* magazine clipping) leave for their first day of classes at Chandler Junior High School in Richmond, Virginia. They were the school's first black students.

have a very deep and lasting friendship. On the first day, we were going in one direction and a horde of photographers stampeded toward us. It was scary. But it was largely peaceful compared to what was going on in other places. No one dragged you out and beat you up. It was more like little tortures each day.

There was name calling, and people would spit on you or trip you up. They would take the tip of their ink pen and squirt ink all over the back of your clothes. You really wouldn't be aware of it until it soaked through to your skin. Lunch was always very messy because they would throw all kinds of things. If someone throws a milk carton that's not empty, when it hits you, it splashes all over you. Afterward you frequently looked like you had swum through your lunch. If any adults saw it, they did nothing. The teachers didn't intervene. They didn't want us there.

The next year we had to start the process all over again in John Marshall Senior High. With a wider range of students, there were more opportunities for hurtful experiences. Gym was particularly horrible because we had to do sit-ups. The other students saw us as contaminated; no one wanted to hold down our feet or have any kind of physical contact. After gym class, we had about 10 minutes to rush into the locker room, take a shower, and change clothes. Everyone was trying to get through a relatively narrow opening in the locker room at the same time. There was a lot of pushing and shoving. If someone accidentally touched Gloria or me, they'd start screaming, "Help, help!" Then their friends would rush up and brush them off.

On Fridays, our gym class went bowling. I had never seen a bowling alley. It was a foreign concept to me. There were no bowling alleys that allowed blacks. The first day when we got to the bowling alley, people went to rent shoes. The teacher told Gloria and me to go down to the other end of the counter and pick up "our shoes"—pink bowling shoes that the Board of Education had purchased in various sizes. That way the owner of the bowling alley could assure his white patrons there was no possibility they might be renting shoes we had worn.

That was a watershed event for Gloria and me, even though we didn't talk about it until years later. As silly and inconsequential as it seems, it just galvanized all our feelings.

When I turned 15, my parents got me a little red Renault to drive to school. The football players would pick up my car and turn it diagonally in the parking space, so I'd have to wait until the cars parked on either side had left. Or they would flatten my tires. Sometimes the football players would trip me in the halls. When I went to pick up my books, they'd laugh and say, "Look at the maid down there scrubbing the floor."

I was always terrified about my grades because my mother had told me that they were going to put my grades in the paper. Although that never happened, little old black ladies—total strangers—would come up to me on the street and say, "We're counting on you to show them that we're smart, that we're human."

One day in biology—my favorite subject—the teacher was introducing the microscope. "Take a hair and practice focusing," she said. I had a microscope at home so I knew what to do, but she came over and said loudly, "Well, your hair isn't like ours!" She said it as though I wouldn't be able to focus the microscope on my different hair.

During one test everyone was cheating, their books open in their laps. The teacher sat on a stool and never took her eyes off me.

Another time, when we had finished a project, she said, "If you want to know your grade, come back after class and I'll tell you." So I went and she said, "Well, you got a C and a D, but since you asked, I'm going to change it to a D and an F." When I told my mother about that, she went to the school and the teacher backed down, saying, "Oh, well, I'm sure I never said anything like that."

There were a couple of white students who tried to be friendly, but they put themselves at risk. When I was in junior high, there was one girl who was friendly when no one was around. But if she was talking with me and someone came down the hall, she would pretend she didn't know me.

I had been selected to integrate the schools because my grades in elementary school were really good. But that worked against me with my black friends. They felt I had been selected because, "Oh, well, you have a high IQ and good grades." That led to jealousy and the false impression that we thought we were better, or smarter, than they were.

That was very hurtful to me. I had been in the same class with these people essentially since kindergarten, and suddenly they weren't my friends anymore. Gloria and I lost all our friends, and we didn't have new ones to fill the void. One black boy's mother made him invite us to a party. Imagine how uncomfortable that was: We were completely ignored, and it was clear that the boy felt, "You're here only because my mother made me invite you."

In my sophomore year in high school, I went to a summer science institute for black students at Virginia Union University and discovered I had a new problem. I'd been taken out of the teenage culture of my own people, and I didn't know their slang, didn't know what were the hot topics, or the latest dance. All of my information about teenage issues was what I had overheard the white kids talking about. I felt like I wasn't a correct fit.

Kids go through this now, in an adolescent culture that says to black kids, "If you speak well, study hard, and do well in school, you're acting white." It puts you in a horrible bind at a time when you're not that mature and the choices you make might not necessarily be good for you in the long term.

What freed me from that was when I realized I wasn't going to fit into either group. So I read a lot. My parents didn't address these feelings, but they made it clear they wanted me to bring pride to my family and be responsible. Sometimes that was very hard. Near my senior year it reached the point where I felt unable to satisfy them in doing all the things they wanted.

My grandparents lived only a block and a half away. When my grandmother died, I went to stay with my grandfather before the funeral so he wouldn't be alone. It was just so comfortable there and we had such a good relationship that I stayed with him the whole year. It allowed me to be a little more independent. He was more accepting than my parents.

My grandfather had really been harmed by Jim Crow. He was very dark skinned. Once he said to me, and I'll never forget it, "How can you love me so much when you're so much lighter than I am?" It was so indicative of the kind of self-hatred, based solely on color, that we nurtured in our people. And it was really internalized: Here was a brilliant and financially successful man, who started several businesses, who owned apartment buildings and his own cab company.

Finding a college was an interesting experience. Gloria and I had this college counselor who told us she didn't understand why we, the black kids, didn't trust her, because she had grown up with the maid's daughter and they were such good friends. When I started going to interviews, I learned that she had sent unsolicited letters to all the colleges that I applied to, referring to me as "it."

I went to Colby College in Waterville, Maine, sight unseen. I'd read about it in *Seventeen* magazine. I wanted to go to school in California, but my mother said no. Maine was about as far away as I could get on the East Coast. I was tired of all the struggles in the South—going into restaurants where people never got around to serving you.

When I moved to New Jersey after college I found the racism was not overt, but it was present. All the things that people in the South were not afraid to say or do go on here, but in a hidden way. When my husband and I were looking for housing, I leafed through the paper and made some phone calls. I called one man who had advertised a two-family house in Summit, New Jersey. His daughter was a teacher and we talked for about an hour. It was like we were old friends—until we showed up. Then it was like "Oh, well, um, uh, it's rented."

That apartment continued to be advertised for about a month. I called him back and said, "If it's rented, why are you still advertising?"

He said, "Well, the ad got stuck in the newspaper's computer, and they couldn't get it out."

I'm a nonconfrontational person, which means I internalize a lot. Whatever I struggle with, I struggle with inside, and it provides an anxiety that may or may not be relevant for every new experience. I always have this feeling, and I don't want to express it to my husband, like, "Oh, well, I'm nervous, we're going into this new situation. Is this going to be a problem?"

Integrating the Richmond public schools was worth it, but as a result of those years I always doubt myself. I don't have the sense of self-confidence that my abilities would merit. If I do something well, it seems to me a fluke.

Would I do it all over again? Yes, but today I'm much older and I have much more experience. I'm probably not as optimistic about changing people as I was at 12. Back then I really thought, "If I'm good, if I do the right things, if I work hard, I'll get them to like me."

It doesn't work.

People used to say, "You can't legislate a lack of hatred, you can't legislate tolerance," and they would use that to fight against integration. They said you couldn't pass a law to make white people accept black people. What they've done is passed laws that regulate behavior, so that the really negative behaviors are not passed on. Maybe they are in some diluted way, but not in a pure form, where white children would feel perfectly within their rights to disrespect black elders, and order them to move off a street.

Is life easier? Yes. The things I worry about, like how I will be treated when I go into a restaurant, white people don't. So the worry may just be my own particular psychological box.

I don't think that ordinary citizens understand the risk they take when a group of people is being demonized. Who knows when your turn will be? I know that people have judged me and acted on those judgments based on no more than what I look like. They didn't know me, they didn't know my name. They didn't even speak to me, but they made a judgment that I was less than human. That I was dirt. That they could treat me in a certain way. That's been true all my life.

ARMS AND HEARTS LINKED
in a common mission, civil rights
leaders form the vanguard of the 1965
Selma-to-Montgomery march.

# II

## WE SHALL NOT BE MOVED

*"God never appears to you in person*

*but always in action."*

**Mohandas Gandhi**

CHAPTER 11

# A BLINDING FLASH OPENED OUR EYES

*The four girls murdered by Ku Klux Klansmen in the September 15, 1963, bombing of Birmingham's Sixteenth Street Baptist Church did not die alone. Other children attended church that morning, including 14-year-old Carolyn Maull.*

*Maull, now 56, still attends the church. Her married name is Carolyn McKinstry, and she volunteers as a guide at the church, patiently answering a perennial question from visitors: Where were you when the bomb exploded?*

THAT SUNDAY MORNING I arrived at church about 9:30 to take my two younger brothers to their classes. At about 10:45, just before the 11:00 service started, I would give the attendance report and the collection report. I liked that little job. It made me feel a part of something important.

So I was coming from downstairs that morning, and when I got to the top of the steps the office phone was ringing.

A voice on the line said, "Two minutes." That was it—not another word. Then he hung up.

Because so many people have asked, I've counted the steps from where I held the phone to where I was when the bomb went off beneath the girls' bathroom. It was about 15 steps.

I heard somebody say, "Hit the floor!" I just fell on the floor with all the stuff I was holding. The explosion sounded like rumbling

RACIAL VIOLENCE reached beyond the horrific on September 15, 1963, with the bombing of the Sixteenth Street Baptist Church in Birmingham, killing *(from top)* Denise McNair, 11; Carole Robertson, 14; Addie Mae Collins, 14; and Cynthia Wesley, 14. A former Klansman was convicted of their murders in 2001.

thunder. I remember thinking there must be a storm outside. As soon as I thought that, the windows started shattering.

Then I heard the sound of many feet. I could hear people getting up, so I did too. We all went out through a back entrance, and once I got outside, I saw a hole in the side of the church where the stairs had been. A crowd had already formed because the rooming houses on both sides of the church had emptied out, and people were everywhere: Police, firemen, people wandering around looking for their relatives.

I went back into the church two or three times looking for my brothers, because they had been downstairs. Every time I went back in, I didn't see them. I remember feeling very frantic.

I found out later that my youngest brother, Allen, had taken off running after the bombing. He ran into the street, grabbed onto the first black man he saw, and clung to his leg. My father was on his way to his weekend job when he got word of the bombing and turned around. As he drove back to town in the direction of the church, he came across my other brother, Wendell.

My dad went back to work that morning after he took us home. At about 4 p.m., we learned the girls had died. The next day the FBI came by the house wanting to interview me.

Four of my close friends had been in the church basement putting on their choir robes, and the explosion killed them all (Denise McNair, Carole Robertson, Addie Mae Collins, and Cynthia Wesley). I learned much later that a fifth girl—Addie's sister, Sarah—had been maimed. Twenty-one others were wounded as well.

The next day I went to school and sat there in a stupor the whole time. Kids said things to me like, "Oh, it's not that bad" and, "Come on, get with it! We've got to go out and play!" Maybe it's a good thing that kids won't let you wallow in stuff too long.

My parents did not talk about the bombing, nor did we talk about it in friends' homes or with their parents. When adults wanted to talk about certain matters back then, they would ask the children to leave the room.

I remember visiting a lot of places with my grandparents and parents, but I don't remember any conversations about the racial situation in Birmingham. I think they probably whispered among themselves about those kinds of things. The problem was, how can they tell you about it without scaring you? If you grow up in a family with lots of love, sometimes you don't know how bad things are. You don't want to share all the horror stories with children until they get a perspective.

My father had a master's degree in physics and chemistry, yet he coped in his own way. After teaching his classes at the high school, he worked a part-time second job as a waiter at the Country Club of Birmingham. By deliberately concealing his erudition from the folks he had to wait on at get-togethers of Birmingham's white elite, he managed to glean a lot of survival tips, and he passed those along to his children.

Even before the bombing, our church rallies had persuaded me to join the student marches. I never even thought about discussing it with my parents, though. I knew they'd worry about me. Plus I knew they were opposed to taking such a direct stand.

One May morning in 1963, I squeezed out through the Parker High School gates and headed downtown with about 200 other students. We paraded toward town and headed toward the church, but because of the police lines and tanks, we ended up at Kelly Ingram Park. Then came the water hoses. "They didn't say anything about water hoses!" I kept thinking: "Where did this come from?"

The water stung like a whip and hit like a cannon. The force of it knocked you down like you weighed only 20 pounds, pushing people around like rag dolls. We tried to hold onto the building, but that was no use.

After it was over, I walked back home. It was dusk, and school let out at 3 p.m., so it was a couple of hours after I should have been at home.

My parents took one look at my appearance—I was still wet, and my sweater was torn—and my father said, "Where in the devil have you been?" I told him.

I didn't really hear what they said to me, but I'm sure they were afraid for me and didn't want to show how much. My father told me I could not go back, that I could not be a part of the demonstrations.

But I could go to church. And if I *happened* to be at the church and somebody *happened* to organize a demonstration, I could join it. He never connected the two.

CHAPTER 12

# JUSTICE NEVER SLEEPS

*William Joseph Baxley was the last person anyone expected to turn Alabama's legal establishment on its head. That's why he was the perfect man to do just that.*

*Baxley's father had been an Alabama lawyer, as had his grandfather before him. So when Baxley was sworn in as the state's attorney general in early 1971, the good ol' boys smiled at each other and nodded approvingly.*

*But not for long.*

WHEN I GOT TO COLLEGE, there was a hard-core group of civil rights activists on campus. It was the time of Freedom Rides and demonstrations, and I felt guilty, like I was wimping out by not joining in. I'd rationalize it by saying, "Well, it ain't going to do any good for me to get beat up." I suppose in some ways I was just a chicken. It bothered me that I wasn't out there.

Then in 1963, when I was in law school, I was having an early lunch at the fraternity house when someone rushed in and said a dynamite charge had gone off at the Sixteenth Street Baptist Church in Birmingham.

That made me sick to my stomach.

There had been so many things that year—Alabama Governor George Wallace blocking Vivian Malone and James Hood from entering the university, the killing of Medgar Evers in Mississippi—but to me this was the worst of all. So I vowed to do something about it.

At the time, I thought they would arrest somebody soon, and I thought that I'd go to the U.S. Attorney or the FBI and volunteer to help with research or bring them coffee or Cokes. It never occurred to me that within a few years I'd be Attorney General of Alabama and could really do something.

The day before I was sworn in, I put the names of the girls who were killed—Cynthia Wesley, 14; Denise McNair, 11; Carole Robertson, 14; and Addie Mae Collins, 14—on the four corners of a state-government telephone card I had been issued. That way every time I used it I'd be reminded of what I needed to do. I took over in January 1971, and within a couple of weeks we had reopened the investigation.

The first suspects we had were J. B. Stoner and his group out of Georgia. It turned out that Stoner had done a lot of bombings, but not the Birmingham one. We found out that Stoner had bombed the Rev. Fred Shuttlesworth's Bethel Baptist Church back in 1958. No one was injured, and the statute of limitations had long since run out, but the church was very close to residents on either side. So we got creative: We charged Stoner not with bombing Shuttlesworth's church but with "setting off explosives dangerously near an inhabited dwelling." He got convicted, and we sent him off for three years.

It was then we found out that Bob Chambliss and his group had been the FBI's suspects from Day 1. We realized we needed the FBI's cooperation to make sure the people talking to us were saying the same thing they'd said before. We also needed the FBI to see if there was anybody we *didn't* know about.

It was a huge struggle to get any FBI documents on the case. I was naïve at the time, so I thought I could convince them. I was a big fan of the yeoman service they'd done in the 1960s. If it hadn't been for the FBI, there's no telling how many other atrocities would have happened. The FBI had good cause not to cooperate with a deep-South law-enforcement agency like mine, I charitably thought, so I was very patient. I let them delay for months in turning over the material. The months turned into years. When FBI Director J. Edgar Hoover died, I thought maybe things would change, but they didn't.

Jack Nelson, who was the *Los Angeles Times* Washington bureau chief, made the difference. Nelson is from Alabama, and a friend of mine, and during a visit to Washington in 1975 he asked if I was still working on the church-bombing case. I told him we were, but that we had just about reached a dead end; unless we got the FBI's help, it looked hopeless.

The next morning he called me really early and said he was going to the Justice Department's public information guy. I never found out if he was bluffing, but he told the guy his bosses had authorized him to do a week-long, front-page series on how the FBI and the Justice Department were blocking the murderers of those little girls from being brought to trial. Nelson called me and said, "Get ready to get a call." Sure enough, the FBI head guy in Birmingham called, saying they were ready to work with us.

I don't fault Hoover's decision not to bring the case against Chambliss back in the '60s. At that stage, with the evidence he had, you had all-male, all-white juries turning people loose who had signed confessions. But I don't know why the FBI refused to cooperate for so long. I could understand if they thought that helping us would compromise their investigation, but it was closed. Their five-year statute ran out in '68.

When I tried Chambliss, one of the people watching during my final argument was a young law student named Doug Jones [the former U. S. Attorney who in 2002 would win convictions against the last two men in the church bombing case]. He decided then, I think, that he wanted some day to deal with these crimes. He's one of my heroes for finishing what I wasn't able to.

*The Birmingham church-bombing investigation turned up evidence in other Klan murders, including the case of Willie Edwards, Jr., a young black Winn Dixie truck driver who disappeared on January 23, 1957. Three months later, Edwards's body was pulled from the Alabama River.*

*In 1976, Baxley—using a confession from a Klansman—filed first-degree murder charges against three men. Eyewitnesses described the final moments in the truck driver's life: The Klansmen had forced Edwards at gunpoint to jump off the bridge and into the river. There were no indictments: The judge, Frank Embry, ruled that "Merely forcing a person to jump from a bridge does not naturally and probably lead to the death of such a person."*

One of my greatest thrills was when I got to tell Willie Edwards's dad that we were getting ready to arrest the people who killed his son. He grabbed my hand and said, "I'm ready to go home now."

I said, "Sir?"

He said he had been praying for God to let him live long enough to find out what happened to his son, and now he was ready to go.

The old man died not long after that, unaware that the case had never gone to trial. Later that year we succeeded in reopening the case, but this time Embry dismissed the charges because the coroner had not determined the cause of death.

When Willie's father had first reported his son as missing, the police did not take him seriously. If there had been an adequate police investigation and an autopsy back then, it might have been different. As it was, Willie Edwards was just another missing person.

People have asked me over the years if I could point to one instance that shaped my views on race, but I can't. All my life I've pretty much felt like I do now. Dothan—the town where I was born and grew up—was relatively progressive as far as civil rights and race relations. Even before I was born, there were African Americans on the police department. Of course, they stayed in the black community, and I'm sure they probably didn't arrest very many (if any) white people, but it was decades before Birmingham and Montgomery did the same thing. The public library in Dothan was open to both races—I didn't know that was unusual at the time. Blacks served on juries and there was no restriction on voting.

Still and all, episodes of discrimination were obvious to me as a child. My parents taught me and my younger brother, Wade, that everybody should be treated with dignity and respect. But when I asked why certain things were allowed to happen, they told me that was just the way things are.

In Sunday school we'd read, "Jesus loves the little children, red and yellow, black and white." Then you'd go outside in the streets, where people weren't treated like that, and you'd ask, "Why?" I've been aware of that contradiction as long as I can remember.

I was in high school in 1956 when riots at the University of Alabama drove Autherine Lucy from campus and she was expelled.

I discussed this with my parents, and they agreed that what had happened to her was wrong. But then they would tell me I couldn't do anything about it—and that I'd ruin myself if I didn't watch out. My dad said that even though it contradicted how he treated people himself.

In 2003, Autherine Lucy, now Autherine Lucy Foster, and I were among the honorees at a ceremony at the university marking the 40th anniversary of the enrollment of Vivian Malone and James Hood. I held her arm as we walked in. The band was playing "Stars Fell on Alabama," and when they turned the spotlight on us I got chill bumps on my arms and tears in my eyes. I thought, "I'm so grateful that I've been allowed to live long enough not only to come to something like this, but to escort this lady in."

CHAPTER 13

# THE VEIL OF AMNESIA

*Diane McWhorter was 10 years old in 1963 when four African American girls died in the bombing of that city's Sixteenth Street Baptist Church. Like many upper-class white students at the time, she remained curiously insulated from the social convulsions of the Civil Rights Movement. At 17, she left Birmingham to attend Wellesley College in Massachusetts.*

*Haunted by questions about the tragedy, McWhorter spent 20 years delving into her past—and into the secrets of her hometown, nicknamed "Bombingham." Her book,* Carry Me Home: Birmingham, Alabama—The Climactic Battle of the Civil Rights Revolution, *won the Pulitzer Prize in 2002. McWhorter's research uncovered collusion between the Klan and the local police, as well as FBI surveillance of the Klan and the Civil Rights Movement. Even so, says McWhorter, 51, she was looking for much more than that when she started the book.*

MY WORST FEAR WAS THAT MY father might be a member of the Klan. My two brothers and I had found Klan literature in his office, crudely mimeographed and printed pamphlets and newspapers. His father was a Harvard Law School graduate; his mother was a Wellesley graduate. They were part of Birmingham society.

But my father was a bigoted Archie Bunker type. He had been a poor student growing up, a bodybuilder who lifted weights to increase his strength. He was a fighter; he wasn't afraid to take people on, and that was his claim to fame. He hung out in beer joints, and in the 1960s he would go out at night saying that he was going to a civil rights meeting. I was afraid he was attending Klan meetings. I would ask my mom, "Where's Papa?" and she would say, "Oh, he's at one of his civil rights meetings." I knew that he carried a gun under his car seat, and I was always afraid that he was going to commit some crime and bring shame upon us all.

I pictured him driving around these bad neighborhoods with his buddies and provoking something. I knew there were a lot of racial bombings in Birmingham, so I guess that's what I thought the Klan was doing. Years later I asked my grandmother, "Why didn't y'all ask him what he was doing?" and she said, "'Cause I was afraid he would tell me."

My father would tell me he was spying on civil rights meetings. I never really found out what he was doing. When I was researching my book and came across rosters of Klansmen, his name did not come up in tens of thousands of pages of FBI surveillance reports. Had he been a member of the Klan, it seems he would've turned up on one of them.

There was a Klansman named Loyal McWhorter, however, and when I came across that name my hands went clammy and my stomach thudded. I thought that was my father, that he would take this kind of romantic name in order to slightly disguise himself. It took me a while to get up the courage to track down Loyal McWhorter. It turned out he was a real person and probably a distant cousin of mine.

I had my moment of truth with my father when I brought the list of Klansmen to him and went through it, saying, "Do you know so-and-so?" I didn't tell him why I was asking. Sometimes he'd say, "Well, sounds familiar." He didn't really know any of them. He didn't deny he was a member back then, but now—since the book has come out and people are asking him about it—he does.

When I talked with him, he was slippery. He would say, "Well, we weren't exactly the Klan." He'd say, "There was Klan plus and Klan minus. We were Klan minus." I thought he might have been part of a front group for the John Birch Society. He also led me to believe that he was a go-between between the Klan and the sons of the powerful industrialists that he had grown up with, who then moved into positions of power themselves in Birmingham. I could not pin him down.

TWO YOUNG WOMEN and a man stand up to high-powered hoses strong enough to rip the bark off trees during a Birmingham demonstration in 1963.

His refusal to deny things was partly not wanting to "disappoint" me by not having a good enough story. That's how perverse he was. His grandiosity was such that he thought I would be happier if he had been a member of the Klan. I think the Klan had an arrested-development type of appeal, where you go out spying on people. I was satisfied that he hadn't taken part in any racial crimes.

Historically, the Klan was not an aberration. It was very much a reflection of the established community. The Klan of the 1930s was a vigilante group to keep labor unions out, to be union busters, when the New Deal threw the authority of the federal government behind the right of workers to organize into labor unions all over the country.

The innovation of John L. Lewis and his newly founded Congress of Industrial Organizations (the CIO) was that it organized across the color line, as his United Mine Workers of America had done. Lewis decided to organize workers by industries as opposed to organizing by jobs (which the American Federation of Labor had done, making it much easier to keep the unions segregated). The CIO's promotion of biracial unionism gave employers the sort of demagoguing gimmick they needed to split the unions racially. So the industrialists initially had vigilantes on their payroll to create racial strife between black and white workers. They published propaganda and anti-Semitic pamphlets to paint the labor movement as an internationalist Communist conspiracy of Jews and their Negro dupes.

During the 1920s, the Klan was actually the insurgent populist wing of the Democratic Party, which had launched the career of Hugo Black as this very liberal Senator who became one of the architects of the New Deal. Black was elected to the Senate in 1926, and it was pretty much the Klan vote that did it. [Later appointed to the Supreme Court, Black became one of its most liberal voices.]

The thing with vigilante groups is that they generally end up disrupting the status quo they were put in place to maintain. That's exactly what happened with the Klan in Birmingham. During the 1950s, our racial strife and segregation jeopardized America's position as a world leader. Racism had been seen as good for the heavy manufacturing industries in Birmingham because it kept wages low, but as the city shifted to a service economy it became bad for business.

The rise of the Civil Rights Movement shined a spotlight on these inequities and injustices. Everything converged in the '50s at a time when the Klan had achieved a life of its own. The Klansmen started operating separately from the establishment that had given their life meaning, that had given them jobs as vigilantes. The establishment tried to put them out to pasture, but it didn't work. They were still bombing houses and beating up on blacks, but they were no longer doing it with the tacit approval of the community leaders, the way it was in the '30s and '40s (and less so in the '50s). By 1963, the Birmingham Klan didn't have much of a following.

As late as 1962, Bull Connor had approved a Klan assassination attempt, with police cooperation, against the Rev. Fred Shuttlesworth, the leading civil rights figure in Birmingham. [As Public Safety Commissioner, Eugene "Bull" Connor was in charge of the city's police and fire departments.] In 1963, Connor was forced out of office when Birmingham's form of government was changed. But he refused to leave. That's what set up the confrontation between Martin Luther King's civil rights demonstrators and Connor's fire hoses and police dogs.

That standoff gave the movement what it needed. Connor was kicked out of office a few weeks after the marches ended in May.

By the time the Klan bombed the church in September, they had lost establishment support. In a way that's why they did it, because the writing was on the wall: Segregation was coming to an end.

*When* Carry Me Home *was published, McWhorter was surprised and moved by the reactions in her hometown. One reason for the acceptance, she felt, was because she was "one of them," a daughter of the South.*

It was a relief to people for the bad stuff to come out. If I'm scolding people, I'm scolding myself as much as anybody, because I was just as bad as anybody else. When the four girls were killed, it was like it happened in a different place. I had no empathy with those girls. The bombing made no impression on me. There had been so many layers of denial in the whole community.

My community operated on a couple of levels. The black world had nothing to do with us. Neither did the redneck white world. The Klansmen were, for us, as much in a different world as the black folks. We thought, "Oh, the rednecks have gotten out of hand and given us a bad name, and we can't do anything about it." You wouldn't approve, but you would say, "Oh, those were just lunatic-fringe people. They don't have anything to do with us."

I never felt hatred toward blacks. I felt condescension. I remember in the sixth grade, a lot of my friends would hem and haw and say, "Oh, you know, I have to admit it, yes, I am prejudiced." I was the class know-it-all, so I said, "Well, you know, I'm a white supremacist, but I'm not prejudiced against them." I thought that was a brilliant moral distinction. It meant that, "Yeah, we're better than they are, but you don't have to be ugly about it. They haven't done anything to you." Even what my father expressed wasn't really hatred. It was vehemence about our way of life coming to an end. He truthfully said, "How can I hate them? They raised me."

I didn't see segregation as my problem. You see this over and over again in our history. You saw it with the Holocaust. As long as it was just the Jews' problem, nobody came to the rescue. When it was just the blacks' problem, the white people who knew better didn't come to the rescue.

I knew better. I knew it was wrong. All the adults knew it was wrong, but they wouldn't do anything. Segregation served their own interests: It's nice to pay somebody to clean your house for a dollar a day.

I saw this a little bit in New York City during the Rudolph Giuliani years. People believed his police were violating people's civil liberties, and that "zero tolerance" was camouflage for whipping up on black people. This didn't really come out until the killing of Amadou Diallo [shot 19 times by four policemen in February 1999 as he reached for his wallet]. We were happy with our "safe neighborhoods." It had served us well.

That was the first time I understood on a visceral level why people I knew hadn't spoken out against segregation, even though they knew it was wrong and violated the principles of our country. Remember, segregation was the law of the land. It was legal. That was the moral hedge. The Supreme Court said it was okay—until the *Brown* decision in 1954, anyway.

When I decided to write the book, I went home and told everyone what I was doing. They were aghast, feigning ignorance about why anybody would possibly want to read a book about Birmingham. They'd go, "Oh, what are you writing about? Hasn't that all been done before? Is there anything new to say? Why can't we forget all that?"

My father gave me this understanding look and said, "Oh, the nigger bit." That kind of sums him up. I just looked at him and shook my head. I went through a long period in my 20s of trying to change him, trying to call him on all the racist stuff. In my 30s I just started taking notes.

What would I have done if I had found out for sure he was a member of the Klan? I probably would've fainted and gone through all the cycles of shock and horror. But I still would have written the book. The drive to find things out would've overwhelmed any kind of emotional inhibitions I might have had about finding out the worst. It would've been devastating. I would've hit bottom, but then I would've known there was nothing worse out there.

Having done the book, I have a real appreciation of the moral complexity of the universe: Good things usually happen not because of altruism, but because people are forced to change. My favorite quote is from Frederick Douglass: "Power concedes nothing without a demand. It never did and it never will." That to me sums it up.

I have a really deeper appreciation of how the world works in certain respects—how people play tricks on themselves, how ideals cover self-interest. Understanding this was like breaking the code of Alabama. I came to see how the haves can advance their interests by making them palatable to have-nots whose own true interests are just the opposite. I came to see how poor people would enter this brotherhood of white supremacy with the rich people, and essentially do themselves a disservice. And how the rich people didn't want to see themselves as bad people.

My fate was being at the wrong place at the wrong time when I was a kid. But it was also being part of a family that I'd tried to reject in so many ways once I left Alabama. When I returned to my family years later, I identified with it and came away with something important—the book. I realized I was the last generation to grow up under segregation, and I'm a witness to that era. And that's my responsibility: Ripping off the veil of amnesia.

*In 1959 Mack Charles Parker—a black man accused of raping a white woman in Poplarville, Mississippi—was dragged from his jail cell by a white lynch mob, beaten, and shot to death. For high-school student Eddie Wilson—now the owner of Threadgill's restaurants in Austin, Texas—that event forced him to make a life-changing choice.*

At first I thought I was supposed to let people around me, my peers, know that I was somehow more prejudiced against blacks than they were. But when Parker was killed, I couldn't picture what I heard had gone on; I couldn't stand knowing that people I knew might have been involved in it.

The summer after that lynching was the year before I graduated from high school, and I had Coach Ox Emerson for a summer-school class on the Civil War. Ox had been really good to me as a football coach the year before. He was different from the other teachers: For starters, he had graduate degrees in history.

That class was the first time a black student had ever been in a class of mine. Early on the first day of the session, I came in and sat down behind the empty seat where the black kid was going to sit. On his desk, someone had left a Venetian blind cord they had made into a little hangman's noose.

Coach Emerson got to class about three strides ahead of the boy. As he walked past the desk in front of me, he saw the same thing I'd seen and scooped it up in his hand. He got to his desk, scribbled something on a sheet of paper, and addressed the black student, who was just then sitting down in that chair: "Would you please go to the office and get me these supplies?"

The young man got up, took the paper from Ox's hand, and walked out of the room.

Ox went livid. He held up the hangman's noose, the veins in his neck popping out. I don't remember exactly what he said, but I do remember that moment as the instant when I realized it was up to me to decide whether to be a good guy or an asshole.

CHAPTER 14

# HEAVEN CAN WAIT

*Joseph E. Lowery was the third president of the Southern Christian Leadership Conference (SCLC), following Martin Luther King, Jr., and Ralph Abernathy. Until he was teenager, he lived in a well-to-do Chicago suburb. Only when he moved with his family to Huntsville, Alabama, did Lowery come face-to-face with the specter of hatred. It was enough.*

ONE DAY WHEN I WAS ABOUT 13, I was coming out the door of my father's little store in Huntsville when this big, burly white policeman was coming in. He punched me in the stomach with his night stick and said, "Get back, nigger! Don't you see a white man coming in the door?"

I ran home to get my Daddy's gun. He was rarely home in the daytime, but for some reason he came home that day and was on the porch when I ran outside with the gun. He took the gun away, and he whipped me for trying to take it. The next day we went downtown to see the police chief, and the chief said there was nothing he could do about it, that it was the only kind of policeman he could hire in Huntsville.

That planted a seed in me. It's a wonder it didn't make me hate. It kind of shaped me, but I never hated. After I went into the ministry, I realized my call to preach involved social justice as much as it did Heaven. I felt called to not only help people make Heaven their home, but their homes here heavenly.

*In the early 1950s Lowery joined other ministers in testing the segregated public transportation laws then in effect throughout the South. This vanguard included not only the Revs. King and Abernathy in Montgomery but the Rev. Fred Shuttlesworth in Birmingham, the Rev. T. J. Jemison in Baton Rouge, and the Rev. C. K. Steele in Tallahassee. Rosa Parks sparked the effort in Montgomery when she refused to give up her seat to a white man.*

The earliest boycotts were in Baton Rouge and Tallahassee, but they were unsuccessful. We used to meet monthly in Montgomery to share our pain, and that was the birth of the SCLC.

Every black person in Montgomery could identify with the humiliation of the buses. Everybody had tasted that bitter fruit or knew somebody who had. It was a personal expression of liberation to boycott.

In Montgomery, I'm confident that God was in the plan, because Montgomery was so ideally suited, for many reasons. The geography and the demographics were significant. Montgomery was not too big and not too small. And the carpools could work; some people could walk. The other thing was that every black person in Montgomery had a personal grievance with the bus line. Even if they hadn't ridden the bus, their mama had this grievance, or their auntie or uncle. Nobody had to use their imagination about what it was like to be abused.

When you add that to the skillful, charismatic leadership that was involved, you have a successful boycott. That's why I say God was in the plan. Martin Luther King and the city were a good marriage.

Then you had the unwitting cooperation of the white leadership. The demeanor of the white folks is what'll determine black folks' response. People like George Wallace and Bull Connor served as reverse catalysts. They were a perfect, understandable target.

Years later, when I was chairman of the MARTA [Metropolitan Atlanta Rapid Transit Authority] board, a white man told me, "How in the hell you figure? Rosa Parks wouldn't have a damn thing to do now, would she? You're chairman of the damn bus system!"

I hadn't thought about it in that light until he said it. I guess that's pretty good progress. A woman had to defy the law to sit where she wanted to, and now a black man is Chairman of the Board of an entire bus company. We've come a long way.

After the success of Montgomery, the NAACP thought that those of us who had been in state leadership positions would come back into the fold—that this fledgling group would just fade away and turn things back over. The tension got so heavy that Clarence Mitchell, Jr., the NAACP man in Washington, wouldn't sit on the platform with Ralph Abernathy at a program somewhere in Maryland because Ralph represented the SCLC.

What really intrigued me was when Martin took Ralph and me to New York to meet with NAACP head Roy Wilkins and Gloster Current, director of branches. In that meeting Gloster said that the only victory from the Montgomery boycott was the court decision [outlawing segregation on buses]. And I said, "Well, now, that's the difference between you all and us: We treasure the court decision, but for us the primary reward was the fact that 42,000 black folks walked here for a year with their feet tired, but their souls rested."

That was the victory—42,000 black folks coming together in unity and solidarity. That's what initiated the whole era of self-determination. People said, "Damn what the courts said. Damn what the legislature said. Damn what the mayor said. Damn what the Congress said. We ain't gonna ride in the back of the bus, that's all there is to it."

And that's when the new Negro was born, a new black was born.

Nelson Mandela told me, "I saw you when they let me see television. I could see you all marching." He said it was amazing how his people expected us to be shot down like they had been in Sharpsville and Soweto. It was inspiring. And it eventually helped them see the efficacy of nonviolence.

Many of our folks never fully embraced nonviolence as a way of life, but they bought into it as a tactic. They had confidence in the leadership, so they would put their weapons down. In 1979 we marched in Decatur, Alabama, on behalf of [mentally retarded felon] Tommy Lee Hines, and Klansmen shot two young black men in the head. We had to go in the church and make everybody leave their weapons.

During that march the Klan shot into the crowd of marchers. The bullet whistled over my head. Two burly guys who were acting as security guards for the march lifted me up by the arms and whisked me out of the way. I was resisting them because my wife was trailing the march in her car. We had gotten the word that the Klan

BERLINERS CELEBRATE as East Germans flood through the Wall in 1989. Many were inspired by the Civil Rights Movement, says the Rev. Joseph Lowery.

was planning something and I didn't want her to march, but when the marchers scattered, there she was alone in the car. They kept shooting and hit the windshield. My wife fell on the seat, with glass falling all over her. She said she stayed there about 10 minutes. It was only about 20 seconds, but it probably seemed like 10 minutes to her. Then she got up and drove off.

The Civil Rights Movement had many offspring. In fact I personally take some credit for the fall of the Berlin Wall. I was invited to East Berlin to preach and to receive a peace award, and the *Atlanta Journal Constitution* sent a reporter over to cover it. I was preaching what I know—dignity of the individual, human rights, freedom—and the reporter came over to me and said, "Doc, don't you think you're being a little heavy on this freedom talk? We may not get out of here. This is a Communist country."

I told him he had watched too many movies. But you know, whenever I'd talk about liberty I could see they were receiving it. And not long after that we saw some of those same folks marching toward the Wall and tearing it down.

That's why I don't let Reagan and Bush take all the credit.

# The Pointed Heel

*In September 1965, Annye Braxton enrolled her daughter Karen as the first black student in the local primary school of Demopolis, Alabama. Both Annye, a secretary at an agricultural extension office, and her truck-driver husband, Charlie, were fired. This was not Braxton's first act of defiance.*

I grew up in Birmingham. I grew up understanding racism.

In 1953, I was a student at Miles College, in the suburb of Fairfield, Alabama, studying natural science. The bus always stopped in front of the whites, but one day the bus driver accidentally stopped in front of the blacks. I got on when he opened the door.

A white man pulled me from the back and said, "Get back, nigger! I get on first!"

I think change comes about when your cup runs over, when you've had enough.

I took off my heel and beat him on his head and face. He was bleeding. The blacks who had been waiting with me disappeared. I had lost a button during the fight and a white woman came to my rescue with a pin to help me close my dress.

The police came and put me in the back seat of a police car and quizzed me. The policeman asked me where did I work, and I told him I was a student. He said, "Well, you're charged with vagrancy because you're not working," and he took me to jail.

My father worked for a lawyer in Birmingham by the name of Beddow. He must have done something because even though I was charged, the case never went to court.

CHAPTER 15

# CRACKING THE SYSTEM

*Raylawni Branch broke the color barrier at three institutions in her hometown of Hattiesburg, Mississippi: the University of Southern Mississippi; the Big Yank textile factory; and the local telephone company. She was also instrumental in integrating the town's Greyhound and Trailways bus stations, and in creating the School of Nursing at USM, where she now teaches.*

*Branch, a working mother of three, views her activism in a much different light than her impressive résumé might suggest. In her office on the university campus, she identified the key ingredient in achieving equality: understanding society's systems and making them work for you.*

WHEN I WAS BETWEEN FOUR and five years old I was already reading, and I decided I wanted to go to school. It was a little three-room schoolhouse with a cafeteria no bigger than this 10-by-10-foot office. The mothers came to school to cook every day and sent jars of peas, cornmeal, or whatever else they could to feed the young 'uns.

One day there was a storm and they turned us out early. But there was no way to let parents know because we didn't have phones. I had to walk down Highway 84 for about a mile, then onto a little dirt road for about a third of a mile, and over to home. It was a Mississippi red-clay dirt road. It was raining so hard that it was just pushing me right down on the ground. I had enough sense to get in the ditch.

I could hear this engine coming down the road. It was a school bus. I guess the white school students were also being turned out early. I had never even seen the school bus on the road. We didn't have school buses; we walked.

The bus was coming along and I got up and started flagging it down. It roared right past, flinging mud and dirt all over me. I got back in the ditch and I cried and I cried. I stayed there until I could hear my daddy's voice. He'd come along the road calling me.

I got up and we went walking home. I said, "Daddy, do you know the bus went right by me?"

He said, "Oh, it did?"

"Yes," I said. "I flagged it but it didn't stop and pick me up."

He said, "Baby, one of these days that bus is going to stop and pick you up."

He did not say to me, "The bus didn't pick you up because you're black." I think that's a bad thing to tell a child. Hypothetically, I expected that bus to stop some day, and I decided that I would make it stop. I don't think change will ever occur unless you take an active role in shaping what's going on.

I'm the oldest of 10 children. Most people owned their own property and had small farms raising peanuts, popcorn. We never said, "Let's go to the store," because there was no such thing as a supermarket at that time. We lived six miles from town. So it was very sheltered.

I first realized there was a difference between the races, however artificial, when I saw the picture of Emmett Till on the cover of *Jet* magazine. That brought it to my attention. Number one, it was from Mississippi. Number two, you couldn't see a worse thing, because the picture *Jet* used was ghastly. It made me start to think.

At Rowan Senior High School, Mrs. Marjorie Chambers—we called her the Hawk—taught world history, and she taught it well. I attribute my political activism to her.

The Hawk taught us how to politic in various clubs like the Tri-Hi-Y. She taught us how to cooperate with other groups in order to get what we wanted. She taught us to compromise. She instilled a sense of pride in us. Among so many of my classmates and me, you won't find that "can't-do" attitude.

As teenagers we listened to the radio and heard the things that Martin Luther King was doing, so we tried emulating that kind of behavior here in Hattiesburg. We did some things to try to stop having to ride in the back of the bus.

Besides being one of the first two black women to attend the University of Southern Mississippi, I was the first to do many things in Hattiesburg. I got married the year I finished high school. And, unfortunately, because I did not know how to work the system, I had no concept of scholarships and grants. I had three young children and a husband who was later diagnosed with paranoid schizophrenia. I went through some real tough times, but I knew I wanted something different.

What made me think about college was trying to get a job. Everywhere you went, you couldn't get a job. You could be a housekeeper, you could work behind the scenes in a restaurant or a cleaner's, but you couldn't do anything else. During high school I worked as a waitress in a black restaurant on Mobile Street. There was no way to get out of that box once you're in it.

One day I got very angry about that. I started looking for jobs, making applications, and fighting back. First I tried Sears, and was hired there as temporary help at Christmas. After that I tried to get hired at Big Yank textile factory, which made work clothes.

I would go to the unemployment office and apply for a job. The unemployment office would send me out to the factory, and the factory would send me back to the unemployment office. One day, I just had it. I virtually climbed up on the desk of the guy at the unemployment office, pointed my finger in his face, and told him, "I know there must be a job up here somewhere! There's a federal job book—I want to see that book!"

They sat me in a room and brought out the book. I'm going through the book, and I'm looking at the qualifications for the various jobs. I had a high school education, but that was it; I had no work experience with anything. That's when I decided I had to go back to school.

After almost a year of trying, I was hired by Big Yank and stayed there about six months. They started an evening shift for four of us black ladies because 400 white women refused to work with us days. The company started making permanent-press work shirts. Once we learned how to run the pressing machines, those 400 women could not cut and sew enough shirts during the day to keep the four of us working for eight hours at night.

I knew that was not for me. I made my desires known to the NAACP and to Robert Beech, the director of the Delta Ministry under the National Council of Churches. Changes were in the air.

In May of '65, there was a young lady, Gwendolyn Elaine Armstrong, who'd graduated from Rowan and wanted to go to school in Hattiesburg because her mother was handicapped and she wanted to stay home and help her. But she didn't want to go to USM as the only black on campus; she was only 18 and afraid of what might happen.

The NAACP asked me if I wanted to go to school, and I just jumped on it. They paid my tuition. I came to school in September 1965.

We had six bodyguards when we came here. The back-room conversation between the governor and school president was, "Hands off. Nothing is to happen to them." We did not have one incident. We spent a lot of time dodging the bodyguards. Then, one day after about six weeks had gone by, we looked up and they were gone.

Because of the time frame and the circumstances occurring all across America, it was probably a whole lot easier to integrate women into the system than it was to integrate the men. I think that's what made the difference here. The same year we came here to USM, two young black ladies went to William Carey College across town, and a cross was burned on President Noonkester's lawn. That did not happen here at USM. Now there's a bronze plaque inside on the wall, commemorating when Elaine and I came here.

They had a big Ku Klux Klan powwow out at Petal, Mississippi, across the bridge from Hattiesburg that first week of school. Elaine and I joked about putting on white sheets and going to the rally. If we were going to die, we said, we might as well know what they're talking about!

I had no counseling, no advisor; I had no money, no day care. I had an 8 a.m. class, and even though I lived two and a half miles from campus, frequently I had to walk. That's where the focus should have been. That I was a working mom trying to go to school at the same time.

For homecoming this past year, they had a big thank-you to the faculty and staff on the campus around the Alumni House, which used to be the president's house. Music was playing and I was dancing on the front porch when I had a flashback: When I was a student, I was working after classes for a professor on campus for 20 hours a week. I made about $1.10 an hour, so I was living on $20 a week. Sometimes I didn't have enough money to take the bus home. One day I was so tired I guess I got crazy. I went up to the university president's house and knocked on the door. The housekeeper—a roly-poly lady named Mrs. Goins, who wore a big white apron—came to the door. She said, "Child, what you want?"

I said, "I'm too tired to walk home today. I came up here to get some bus fare from the president."

Maybe I'd had a nervous breakdown, I don't know. But she went in her pocket, handed me a quarter, and said, "Here, child, you go home." I will never forget her.

I did not grow up with fear, and once I learned how to work the system, I was not afraid to ask. For that entire year, my children and I ate whatever canned goods we were given. The rent for my little two-bedroom house was $20 a month. I had lights, gas, water, and telephone bills and three babies, ages 6, 5, and 3. By the time I paid the milk company, paid my bills and my rent, I didn't have anything left out of that $80 a month.

I would never have thought of going on welfare because that just wasn't part of your mentality. Only poor folks went on welfare. When I look back at it now, I was stupid. But I never did.

I had been trying to get into a nursing program run by the Methodist Hospital here in Hattiesburg, but it was segregated. You couldn't sue the church at that time. I found out that USM had some connection with the school, so we thought we could bring a suit against USM to prevent them from getting federal funding. After meeting with the dean of women at USM, I decided I would not sue, and they promised to open a school of nursing—which they did, in '67.

I got a scholarship to go to nursing school in New York. After that I joined the Air Force and eventually worked my way up to lieutenant colonel in the Air Force Reserve.

I've always made a point to do things that I was afraid to do. For example, I stayed on active flying status with the Air Force for many years, even though I was deathly afraid to fly.

No change comes voluntarily.

*For a certain generation of Americans, the desegregation of public schools hit with a shock. Between fistfights, however, Ron Kirk learned some valuable cross-cultural coping skills that later helped him become the first black mayor of Dallas.*

I'm the youngest of four children. We all had the experience of beginning life in a segregated school system, and all of us were part of that first wave to go and integrate. In my case, it was University Junior High in Austin, Texas.

My first experience in an integrated environment was very much an experiment—intentionally one-third Hispanic, one-third African American, and one-third Anglo—and we went through all the emotions and trauma you would expect for kids lumped together at that time of their lives and that time in our history.

We all got along, but there were skirmishes. I don't know that we ever had riots, but there were lots of fights, and they always involved girls—you know, somebody talking to a girl from the "wrong" ethnicity. Once a month or so we'd have a big rumble. The Hispanics and the Anglos would gang up to beat up the black kids, or the blacks and Hispanics would gang up to beat up the white kids. There was a certain amount of democracy, because it moved around.

The curious thing was this: After a day of all of us struggling to make this whole desegregation thing work, we would walk home and run into neighborhood friends, and they would ridicule us and want to fight us because we were going to school with white kids. So in the course of a single day we might get beat up because we were black, then get beat up again because we weren't black enough!

CHAPTER 16

# LOUISIANA MOON

*Maurice Edwin "Moon" Landrieu, 73, was mayor of New Orleans from 1970 to 1978. He is now the proud parent of a Louisiana political dynasty, including his daughter, U.S. Senator Mary Landrieu. He came close to never making it that far: After people discovered that Landrieu had been a secret supporter of integration, he barely survived his first term as a Louisiana state legislator.*

*That revelation came to light only when school desegregation boiled to the surface. Despite the racist attitudes of many of his supporters, Landrieu could do only one thing. And that was the right thing.*

WHEN I FIRST RAN FOR OFFICE, I knew I couldn't go around saying I was for integration. I wouldn't have gotten elected in Louisiana in a million years. This was in 1960, before civil rights, when most whites were overwhelmingly in favor of segregation. But I decided I was not going to promote segregation.

Nobody in my family had ever been in politics. I was feeling my way the entire time. When I was running for office, one senator told me, "Listen, son, we just want to give you some advice. You've got to put two things on the campaign hand cards you give out: Number one, you're against any increase in taxes; and number two, you're for segregation."

I didn't put either one on my card. I got elected and the first important measure that came up in the Legislature was the reconstitution of the State Sovereignty Commission [a watchdog agency devoted to preserving racial segregation in the state]. I raised my hand and said, "I object."

There was dead silence. Then I was asked, "Mr. Landrieu, what is your objection?"

I said, "Well, I don't know anything about it. Would somebody please tell me what this thing does and why we need it?"

This is like jumping in front of a freight train. After the legislature let out, I went back to the hotel lobby, and there I was standing right behind Leander Perez [the segregationist boss of Plaquemines Parish] and state legislator Willie Rainach, who had run for Governor on the segregation ticket. Rainach put his finger on my chest and he said, "We know your kind and we're gonna get you."

Of course I was scared. But I said to him, "Take your best shot"—a bravado kind of thing. I was only 29 years old. They went into the hotel, and after my hands quit shaking and I calmed down a little bit, I said, "Hey, these guys are serious."

Then came the local *Brown v. Board of Education* court order to integrate public schools in New Orleans. The school board had a referendum, and the public voted overwhelmingly to close the schools rather than integrate them. The board was shocked. Abandoning public education was worse to them than the concept of integration.

They came up with a "pupil placement" concept. They took schools in poor white neighborhoods where you also had blacks, saying they were economically the same, and decided to integrate the two. All hell broke loose. Of course there were demonstrations. The town was not burning down—this was not Watts, or Detroit, or Washington. They were just ugly people down there screaming at the black kids as they walked to school. The marshals walked the kids into school. And Governor Jimmie Davis had called the legislature into special session.

I had to make up my mind at that point. I desperately wanted to be in public office. I didn't want to lose what I had so arduously worked for and miraculously obtained, but how far out front was I going to be with my racial attitudes?

No one ever told me segregation was morally wrong when I was growing up. It was just a fact of life. You grew up in this white world not actively thinking or believing or caring, frankly, about the fact that blacks were deprived or cheated. That's just the way the South was back then.

My mother was a marvelous human being, but not an educated woman. She wasn't an actively aggressive, hating person. But one day I told her blacks were as good as I was, and she said, "Don't ever say that. It's not so." My mother was born in 1903 and had lived in the aftermath of Reconstruction. She interacted with blacks on a daily basis in the store that was in the front room of our house, and she was very kind to them, giving them credit when they didn't have money. But credit did not mean equality.

I thought one day I'd be President of the United States, as every 29-year-old who gets elected for the first time thinks. My future's ahead of me. And I was worried to death about going against the segregationists, to be honest with you. I remember going to church and praying for the right decision. Because I knew what was coming up at Davis's special legislative session as soon as I walked in those doors. And I walked out of the church with the resolve that they couldn't eat me, so let's go.

The trick was to be nimble enough and still not lose your soul, to stay alive politically and still make the case. You could bare your chest and say, "Here I am, kill me!" And they *would* kill you, and what do you do with that? Nothing, you're dead. I'm not saying it's a useless sacrifice, because there'll be other people walking over your body.

My role model was St. Thomas More, a heroic figure in the history of the Catholic Church. In opposing Henry VIII's divorce and marriage, he used his intelligence; he didn't go out and defy the king. He resisted in every legal way he could and used his knowledge of the law to defend himself. But in the final analysis, when it got down to an issue that was so narrow he had to say yes or no, More said no. Then they chopped his head off.

I've always thought that was a remarkable performance on his part. He did it with such great intelligence, yet sacrificed nothing of what he was as a human being until the final issue. I thought a lot about him and said, "Look, use your head, be smart, be clever. Leander Perez, Willie Rainach and the other 'segs' just want to destroy you."

In fact, Loyola University's St. Thomas More Law Society had been the scene of my most personal encounter with racism.

In 1952 Loyola had admitted the first two African American guys to the law school. Before that, segregation was faceless. It was blacks and whites. All of a sudden I meet up with Ben Johnson and Norman Francis, and they were two nice guys, clearly no different from me. They dressed better than I did, coming to school every day in coats and ties. And clearly they were just as smart, if not smarter, than I was.

They made segregation look stupid. You grow up in Southern society with all kinds of crazy myths: "Blacks are lazy; blacks are dumb; blacks are hard-headed. If you get into a fight with one of them, you got to hit him in the shin, 'cause their head's so hard." Those myths got dispelled when I met Ben and Norman.

There may have been one or two guys who didn't want Ben and Norman to join the law club at Loyola, but we blew them off. When it was time to have our annual social event, we found out there was no place we could go because of Ben and Norman. I'm not talking about Antoine's or Galatoire's, just a little neighborhood restaurant. So I got a bunch of crayfish, we all put up a few bucks to pay for it, and we had it in my backyard.

The next day my mother said, "You know last night, when that big colored man came to my door, I was shocked." She was talking about Ben Johnson.

She said, "I just didn't know what he was there for, and I felt embarrassed."

Well, she let him in because he said he was there for the party. I sensed what my mother was saying: For the first time in her life, a black man had knocked on her door not as a salesman or a workman or someone looking for a handout, but as a guest in her home.

So I said, "Mom, gee I'm sorry. I should've told you."

She said, "Yes, you should have."

I said, "But would it have many any difference to you?"

She said, "No, but you should've told me."

It's hard to understand unless you lived through it. Here's a good soul—a fair, decent, honorable person—who, having been raised in a certain culture all her life, had never had a black person come socially to the house. On the other hand, she was not advocating to hold back the flood, like George Wallace.

I wanted to change the world, not just racially, but to make the world a better place. I had this flame burning inside me to make a difference in the world. I can't tell you where it came from. I just knew you could change the system, not in giant movements but like termites eating away at the pillars of homes in New Orleans.

I've gotten an enormous amount of credit for having stood up and been heroic during my years in political office. I don't feel that way at all, and I'm not being overly modest. I took some chances, but by and large I think I was smart enough and disciplined enough not to give my enemies any reason unnecessarily. I've been called a Communist, a "nigger-lover"—you name it. I learned to live with that. I survived and three years later got re-elected to the State Legislature.

Then I went on the offensive. I had been re-elected, the schools had been integrated, and the world hadn't come to an end. Jimmie Davis was no longer in office. I reintroduced the Compulsory School Attendance Law, which said every child of a certain age has to attend school. We had repealed that when we said we're not going to make you send your child to integrated schools.

I introduced a bill to simplify the voter registration form, which was very complex, designed to keep people from registering. Bear in mind this is 1964, before the federal Voting Rights Act. The more I did, the more whites—not all whites—spat at me, and the more blacks loved me. It became easier for me to do more and more. Then I ran for Councilman-at-Large in New Orleans; once I got elected (in May of 1966) and became president of the City Council, I had more direct power than being just one of 101 legislators dealing with a conservative governor. So I took small steps. But segregation was still out there.

The very first day, I got a black to say the opening prayer in the City Council meeting. You might say, "Well, how big is that?" I don't know, except it had never been done before. Then I took the Confederate flag out of the City Council. I saw it as an abusive symbol to blacks and had it removed at night. Again, doesn't sound like much, but South Carolina didn't take down the Confederate flag from its state capitol building until 2000.

I also took down the United Nations flag. The segregationists came in and demanded to know who had taken down the Confederate flag, and under what authority. I said there was no authority for it to be there to start with. I said there would be three flags flying when the City Council is in session: the flags of the United States, the state of Louisiana, and the city of New Orleans.

As mayor, I tried to be smart and appoint good people. Then I found myself being criticized by some of my black friends, who said, "All you want are super-Ns." I said, "Yeah, you're right. It doesn't do me a damn bit of good to replace an incompetent white with an incompetent black."

People like to talk about equality; they somehow think that if blacks were in a position of authority, they would be different. But we're blind if we think that people are interested in equality for everybody. We're interested in equality for us. There were times when I said to leaders from black organizations, "Get me a person for this job" and they didn't have one, but they'd rather see the job go vacant than have a black from another group get it.

What surprises me the most is the intransigence of racial issues. Although vast changes have been made, sometimes I wonder whether the world at large will ever really change that much: race discrimination, religious discrimination, hostility of all kinds. It's better than it was, but it's not perfect. And it troubles me that we can't grasp the idea of everyone living in peace as brothers and sisters.

I remember on the day *Brown v. Board of Education* was announced saying, "Thank God, it's over. Segregation has ended."

That was 50 years ago, and we're still going through it. Maybe we have to readjust our goals. I don't see us getting there right away, in terms of living in peace and harmony, sharing what we have, being fair. But what else is there?

## *The Best Revenge*

*Ruben Bonilla Jr., a past national president of the League of United Latin-American Citizens, learned at a young age how to outsmart racists.*

My mom and dad were both Mexican citizens, so my entire family is first-generation American. My dad arrived with a third-grade education. He moved from job to job, pretty much as a grunt laborer. He began working at a little gas station and took over when his boss, Monroe Miller, left the business. My dad sent all eight children to college on the gas station income.

When I was six, my mother made me a little Texaco uniform. My job was to clean the headlights and the taillights with a rag and sweep out the cars. Back then a quarter tip was a lot of money, and I could make five bucks in a day. That was my savings.

I remember Mr. Judkins calling once. Back in those days, you'd call the operator to make your call. The operator said, "Hold for Mr. Judkins."

Mr. Judkins said, "Let me talk to that wetback." I didn't know what he was talking about, so he persisted.

"The Mexican man. I need the Mexican, boy."

I knew he was talking about my dad. Even at that age I was shocked. It's something that stayed with me all these years. Albert Judkins was a well-respected gentleman rancher and community leader, but his attitude was fairly typical of the Calvert mindset of that era.

My dad said, "Don't worry about it, son. He has to pay us for his gasoline, and he has to pay us for his oil. You're going to go to college on that money."

He made me realize that, in essence, we were the ones exploiting Mr. Judkins. Our prices were good, and even though he hated to associate with Hispanics, he had no choice but to shop with us.

CHAPTER 17

# WAKE UP, WASHINGTON!

*The great civil rights marches of the 1960s demanded intense preparation. At the heart of many of them—particularly the 1963 March on Washington for Jobs and Freedom—was Rachelle Horowitz. A rebel to the bone, she found a way to focus her activist streak the day she met charismatic civil rights leader Bayard Rustin.*

BAYARD RUSTIN AND ELLA Baker were running this office called "In Friendship" on West 57th Street in New York, raising money and arranging demonstrations to support the Montgomery bus protest. Jackie Robinson was scheduled to speak at a rally, and they had printed up thousands of leaflets—with the wrong dates. These were the old days, right? 1957. Bayard was sitting there with a black crayon, changing the dates by hand, so that's what we did—we sat there with him and changed the typo.

I was overwhelmed by Bayard and Ella. They would sit in that two-room office at In Friendship and talk about what was going on in the movement. One of them would say, "By the way, you should read Melville Herskowitz on the Negro history." We devoured their suggestions—it was a second college education.

They would talk and joke, then get up and take calls from "Martin" down in Montgomery. I thought, "At last, here are two people who are going to change the world for the better."

I had rebelled fairly early in life. My family was pretty

APOSTLE OF PEACE Bayard Rustin organized the August 1963 March on Washington for Jobs and Freedom and shared with Martin Luther King, Jr., his teachings on the philosophy of nonviolence.

dysfunctional—I was raised by my divorced mom and grandmother. If there's anything that saved me, it was the public schools. You'd have to tie me down to keep me from going.

When I got to Brooklyn College, I became friends with all the campus rebels—the NAACP people and the ADA [Americans for Democratic Action]. I became a Democratic Socialist—that is, opposed to the Soviet Union but opposed to capitalism. We students were organizing demonstrations in support of the Montgomery bus protest; Tom Kahn and I went over to help Bayard, who had been developing an activist, nonviolent wing of the Civil Rights Movement.

He was planning the Prayer Pilgrimage, a demonstration for integrated schools in Washington, D.C., that would bring together all the ministers who had contact with Dr. King and take the movement national. To get the Prayer Pilgrimage mobilized, we had to get buses to take people to Washington, and we had to get leaflets out.

Bayard was explicit: "You will charter three buses. You will tell them to leave from here. You will—" He and Ella began to teach us about nonviolence, and discipline, and direct action. They were running very disciplined shops. I understood why. Our goal was to get national support. And to get people to support you, you had to make what you're doing compelling.

He had a theory he called "social dislocation." Years later he modified it, but back then it went basically like this: "If there are buses or segregated institutions, and black people make it impossible to use those buses or institutions, you want to have the majority say, 'Okay, we will integrate them.'" But at the same time that you were making life uncomfortable for people, you had to make it as attractive as possible for them to come around to your side.

Bayard knew that police brutality was serious, but he would joke, "Every time 10 black people gather on a street corner, people think it's a riot." So that the police wouldn't overreact, you had to convince them it was not a riot. Nonviolence was necessary for both reasons—to draw public support and to keep the police from overreacting.

After the *Brown* decision, the struggle had to go to Washington, it had to go to federal legislation, and it had to go to the courts. It all started with the 1957 Prayer Pilgrimage—and culminated with the March on Washington.

The March on Washington was organized in eight weeks, but it was thought out for six months. In the winter of 1963, Bayard, Norm Hill, and Tom Kahn drafted a memo to A. Philip Randolph: "Let us have a march on Washington for jobs." What Bayard saw then, obviously, was that the Civil Rights Movement for integration could go only so far without economic integration. Randolph started circulating the memo to Roy Wilkins, Whitney Young, Dr. King, and Jim Farmer, and it sort of hung around, you know? Then the demonstrations began in Birmingham, and in Jackson after Medgar Evers was killed.

It took months and months to gather the support of civil rights leaders for this proposed march. By the time they all met with Randolph and agreed, they had added "for Jobs and Freedom" to the title. Kennedy had just introduced the Civil Rights Bill, and the situation had changed. Bayard was convinced, and I think Randolph was too, that without a march like this in the summer, without something to mobilize black people, there were going to be riots all over.

I was the transportation coordinator. I learned all about chartering buses and getting them to the various groups. I made sure every bus had a captain, and I recorded their name and address on index cards so we could send them the plan of the day. We marched like an army.

We had opposition. The hardest part came from our friends in the Kennedy administration. President Kennedy was scheduled to go to Europe, and the attorney general was terrified at the prospect of his absence during riots. There was this terrible stereotype that when black people come to Washington, the town is going to be ripped up.

The Kennedy administration got all these liberal senators who had been civil-rights advocates to write letters to Randolph and King, saying, "You don't want to come to Washington—there'll be riots. How are you going to handle it? There won't be enough latrines."

We called them "toilet letters." They came from people like Hubert Humphrey and Paul Douglas, all these great liberals.

Then there was the day that South Carolina Senator and staunch segregationist Strom Thurmond tried to attack Bayard, who was gay, by saying that "a queer Communist" was leading the march.

Every so often we would have to scale things down. For instance, we were going to march around the White House. When the Kennedys agreed to allow the march, they said we couldn't do that.

Every so often, Bayard would try to explain to the hotheads among us, "It's really all right. Even if we march in a circumscribed area, if we get 250,000 people to Washington, it doesn't matter."

This is the story I love to tell. When I had been to Washington on youth marches, both times I couldn't find my bus and wandered around lost. So I said to Bayard, "Listen, when we bring these buses in, they have got to park where they drop people off on the Mall, or else people are going to get lost."

But Bobby Kennedy and the entire regalia of the Justice Department told Bayard that the usual procedure was for the buses to drop people off, then park someplace else. They had never been allowed to park near the Mall. Bayard, who could affect a great British accent, later told me that he said, "My transportation director has explained to me that if these buses are moved there will be riots."

I think it was the only march in the history of the United States when the buses weren't moved after they had dropped off their passengers.

Being 22 gives you a certain amount of chutzpah in this world, right? I carefully calculated how many people would be on the march, and came up with something like 88,752 people, because I knew exactly who had chartered planes, buses, and trains. I managed to upset everybody because that was less than 100,000.

Bayard took my number to a meeting of the big six—the chairmen of the march—and NAACP Executive Director Roy Wilkins said, "Bayard, we're home free, because she hasn't factored in who's coming on public transportation. She doesn't know who's driving by car, and she certainly doesn't know who'll wake up in Washington that morning and say, 'Hey, I'm going to the march!'"

Wilkins was right. At least 250,000 people were there.

After the march, we had a week of euphoria. We knew we had to pass the Civil Rights Bill. We started working on organizing marches on state capitols. Then we started working on establishing a permanent organization for Bayard.

A week later the Sixteenth Street Baptist Church was bombed, and we went—*swoop!*—down the tubes. So much for euphoria!

I went to Jackson, Mississippi, to work on voter registration and plans for the upcoming 1964 Freedom Summer, which Bob Moses later asked me to coordinate. It was indescribably terrifying and horrible. Right after I arrived I was walking down the street, and this big white cop with guns on all sides stopped me and said, "So you're the new girl Moses brought in, huh?"

Talk about surveillance! We were told we couldn't move. We couldn't leave—we couldn't walk down the street by ourselves. We could stay on the black block, but we couldn't go into the white area. After living in that atmosphere for a while, the fear would sort of subside: You walked around not knowing how afraid you really were.

The more I stayed and participated in the discussions, the less I thought a white woman should be coordinating it. I felt that the SNCC offices—particularly in Mississippi—were really the only places in the South where black kids could run their own show. When you superimposed these smart-ass white Northerners, it set up resentment.

The second problem that Moses had is that the only way he could get any attention in Mississippi was to bring in white kids with affluent families and ties in the North. If white kids got hurt, went the thinking, people will pay attention. But what did that say to the black kids there? "Your lives aren't worth as much, and those in the movement know it." I understood it clear as a bell. It wasn't hard to figure out why local kids resented Northern whites—who, after all, could always leave.

To be thoroughly honest, I really preferred to work in the North with Bayard. So I said to Bob, "I just don't think I should do this. I think it's a bad idea. I'm going back." When those three kids [Michael Schwerner, Andrew Goodman, and James Chaney] were killed, I was horrified. They were killed in a car we used all the time. I thought, "Oh, my God, am I glad I didn't send them out."

In fact, neither Bob nor Dave Dennis of CORE ever fully understood the danger of the project or the personal toll it would take on them. In retrospect, I think it's terrible there were no adults around to say, "What are you kids doing here? Do you understand the implications?"

When I left Jackson, I took a plane to Birmingham, and when it landed I thought, "Whew, do I feel better!"

About 15 years ago I returned to Jackson to speak to the American Federation of Teachers. It was so different. The hotel where I stayed was integrated, and so was the local union. I began my speech by saying, "When I was here in 1963 as a civil rights worker, I couldn't come into this hotel."

Everyone in the audience—the blacks and the whites—looked at me as if I were from Mars.

*Quentin Mease, a social worker who ran the "colored" branch of the Young Men's Christian Association (YMCA) in Houston, remembers a pivotal moment in the process of reshaping the city's racial politics.*

In February 1960, around the time the sit-ins began in North Carolina, we were setting up for this NAACP banquet when Eldrewey Stearns, a law student at Texas Southern University who worked part-time at the Y, saw what we were doing. He had always been a feisty youngster, and he got up on the dais and recited the Gettysburg Address into the microphone.

"How did that sound, Mr. Mease?"

I was a little vexed, because we were trying to work, so I said, "That sounds all right, but I think you could serve a better purpose if you and those other students up at TSU emulated what they're doing over there in North Carolina." What I was saying was, "You're up there fooling around, but you're not doing anything in Houston."

Eldrewey didn't say anything.

The next day when he showed up for work, he came and stood in my office door. I looked up. "Well, Eldrewey?"

He said, "I want you to meet the president of the PYA."

"The PYA—what's that?"

"The Progressive Youth Association," he said.

"Well," I said, "What is the Progressive Youth Association?"

He said, "It's a sit-in organization in Houston."

"Sit-in?"

"Uh-huh."

I said, "You've got a name and you've got a president. When are you going to sit in?"

The next day came the word that 17 TSU students had staged a sit-in at the lunch counter of Weingarten's grocery store on Almeda Road. Rather than serve the students, the store had closed. The sit-in had been led by Eldrewey Stearns.

CHAPTER 18

# THE BRUTAL TRUTH

*As an award-winning Southern journalist, Karl Fleming covered the worst of the civil rights era, experiencing personal danger and emotional turmoil.*

*After a miserable childhood of abandonment and abuse, Fleming thought he knew a lot about enduring life's injustices. Then he became a newspaper man—and came face-to-face with the brutal truth about how public officials conspired against an entire race.*

I CAME OUT OF MAUL'S SWAMP, North Carolina—the Deep South, the redneck South, Erskine Caldwell's *Tobacco Road* country. We lived in dire poverty in a shotgun shack. My father died when I was five months old. My mother struggled, trying to sell dishes and Bibles door-to-door. Finally, in desperation she married my father's best friend—the two had sold insurance to tenant farmers. My stepfather was significantly older and he soon got ill and died. My mother got tuberculosis and was placed in a state institution.

As for me, I got sent off to the Methodist orphanage in Raleigh, North Carolina, at age eight. That's where I grew up. It was a harsh, isolated environment. We had a 300-acre farm and an 80-cow dairy herd. We worked on the farm every day and went to school, too. It was rigidly disciplined; there was no parental or familial affection of any kind. It was, to use a Southern expression, "Root, hog, or die!"

I was a sensitive and shy little kid. My nickname was Pretty Boy. A kid named Fatty Clark kicked my ass every day. The orphanage had a library of about 3,000 books. I think I read every one. That was my hiding place, my refuge from the tough atmosphere. I especially loved Dickens and Mark Twain. From them I got my passion about social injustice and my appreciation for the beauty of language and imagination. Those guys were my heroes.

I came out of the orphanage with a lot more anger than I understood I had at that time. I had, in effect, been given away by my mother, and put in a tough place. I turned pretty cynical, pretty bitter. On the other hand, that experience was probably the genesis of my liberal attitude as a civil rights reporter; I instinctively took the side of the underdog. I identified with the powerlessness of black people because I was so angry about my own life.

I have a vivid memory of my first real consciousness of racism. There was this old black guy named Tom Roach who worked on the farm with us. He was the ditch digger—he could plow a really straight line, and he could cut a really straight ditch. He did those highly skilled things, but he made very little money.

The farm boss was a tough Scotsman named Mr. Russell. Some days it would rain and we would sit around in the milk barn, waiting for it to quit raining and watching Mr. Russell smoke these noxious cigarettes. Tom Roach would come up and amble back and forth, very uncomfortable. Mr. Russell knew what he wanted, but he always made him beg for a cigarette. Everybody would laugh. I was only nine years old, but I remember feeling aligned with Tom Roach, who had been humiliated in this way.

My mother, self-absorbed though she was, was not a racist. She was very different from the people around her. She made no distinction between white people and black people; she was very polite with black people, although she rarely had anything to do with them. At the orphanage everyone used the word "nigger" quite freely. Across the road was a big woods, and on the other side of that was "Nigger Town." We would go and have rock fights with these kids. They would call us "soda crackers" and we would call them "niggers." That's just the way the world was.

I ran off and joined the Navy when I was 17, just at the end of

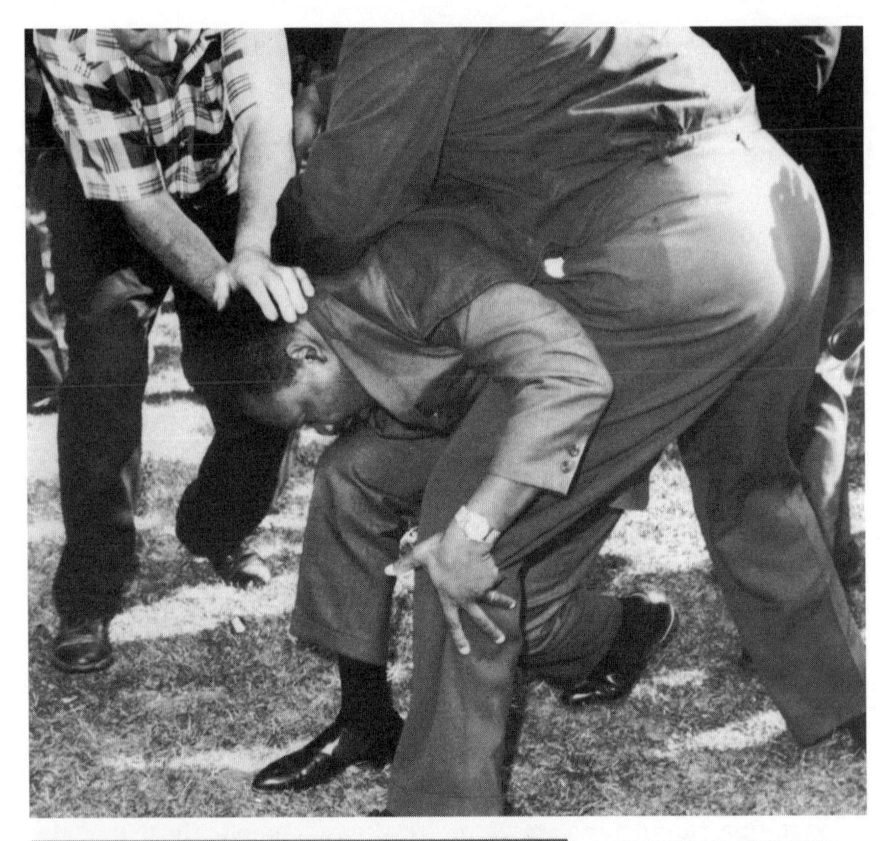

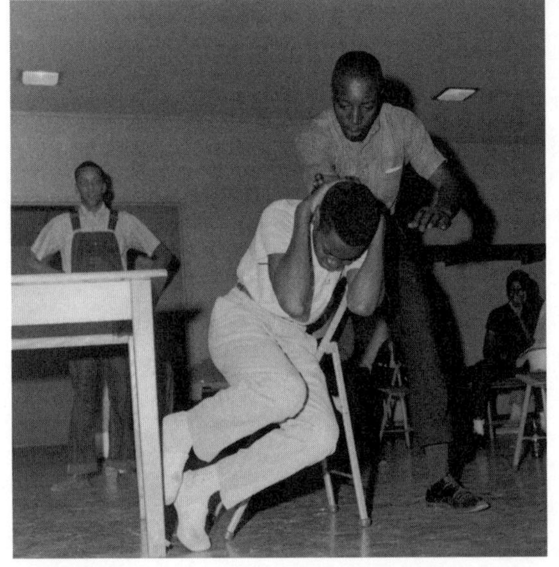

HIS SPIRIT UNBENT, Martin Luther King, Jr., demonstrates the art of passive resistance after being hit by a rock during a march in Chicago. At left, CORE field worker David Dennis, 22, assumes an anti-rabbit-punch position during training at the group's School of Nonviolence in Jackson, Mississippi.

World War II, then went to Appalachian State Teacher's College on a football scholarship. I became a newspaper reporter—and loved it. For a kid like me, journalism seemed a way out. I did not have a good education; I did not come from a good family; I did not have the background or opportunities that might have been open to more privileged kids. But a newspaper was a meritocracy: Nobody cared what your background was—it was how well could you do, and I did very well. Plus I had a dawning sense of moral outrage at the injustices I saw. By illuminating these things, I thought you could change them.

My first city editor was Jim Fulgum. One day I got a call from the coroner: "Karl, there's been a nigger killing out in the country if you want to go." I told Fulgum, and he said, "I'd better go with you."

It was my first murder case. We rode out to this place on the edge of a corn patch in the woods. As we got out of the truck and walked over, we could see a couple of deputies standing around an ambulance. Nearby lay this black woman on her back, contorted, cotton dress up around her thighs, barefoot with a huge gash around her throat, flies all over, a big puddle of blood.

Sitting on a stump was this black guy, and a bloody butcher knife lay nearby. The sheriff said, "They was drinking and dancing over at this juke joint, and they got into a fight and he cut her th'oat."

I thought I would throw up. I said, "Well, that'll be a lesson for her." Fulgum looked at me. They put the guy in a car and took him to jail. Fulgum took me aside. "Don't ever let me hear you say anything like that again," he told me. "That was a human being on the ground."

I had been trying to cover my fear—my revulsion at the loss of a human life—by making a cynical remark. I learned a big lesson that day.

I used to ride the back alleys with a big tough police detective named Ray Hartis. "Come on, kid," Ray would say as I walked by the police station. "Let's go for a ride." We would drive across the tracks and cruise past the shotgun houses of "Nigger Town" and all the black people would bow and scrape: "Good evening, Mr. Hartis." "How you doing, Mr. Hartis?"

He would pull up to the window of two black bootleggers. Someone would hand him a bottle of booze. Then he'd ask, "What's going on?" If there had been any robberies or break-ins—if anybody had any extra money—these two would be the first to know, because the thing to do with extra money was buy whiskey. That was how he kept tabs on what was going on.

One night when we were riding around, he stopped in front of this shack and got out. I said, "Where you going, Ray?"

He said, "I heard this son-of-a-bitch belongs to the NAACP."

I said, "Oh," and got out of the car and followed him. He opened the screen door and walked right in without knocking. Inside was this plain living room—chest of drawers against the wall, pictures of Jesus and Roosevelt on the wall. He began to open the drawers.

I said, "What are you doing?"

"I'm looking for the son-of-a-bitch's NAACP card," he said.

This old black guy came out of the bedroom, pulling on his overalls and saying, "Evening, Mr. Hartis, you got a search warrant?"

Ray turned and slapped him across the face, and down on the floor he went. Hartis said, "That's one side of my goddamn search warrant. You want to see the other?"

Back in the car, I was too shocked to say anything.

What came next was a long dissertation on the character of "niggers"—the same cruel Southern talk I would hear many times in the ensuing years: They are not quite human; they are stupid; the bullet-headed nigger is different from the blue-gum nigger, blah, blah, blah. As a young reporter, I had found black people to be extremely wary if you went into their community. Well, that night I learned why: It meant trouble with a capital T.

In 1960, I went to work for *Newsweek* in the Atlanta bureau. My colleague, a perfectly nice Southern gentleman, was not much turned on by the civil rights story, so it became mine. There was a bunch of bright, adventurous, and socially conscious young guys in the New York headquarters, led by Osborn Elliot, an Eastern-tweedy editor who recognized the historical importance of this story. He turned me loose on it.

The Southern newspapers did not cover the story of the Civil Rights Movement at all. *The Atlanta Constitution*—the biggest newspaper in the South—ignored both the James Meredith story in 1962 and the Birmingham protests in 1963. The papers that did cover them, with some exceptions, were extremely racist. My opinions were well known, and all the local rednecks, the sheriff, and everybody else identified me as a member of the "Yankee, Jew, Communist, nigger-loving press," and a traitor to "our Southern way of life."

My good friend Claude Sitton lived in Atlanta and wrote for *The New York Times*; that paper and *Newsweek* magazine were about the only major publications regularly covering the story. We were harassed all the time. It was very scary. We covered voter registration drives and sit-ins. We'd get a rental car, and he would drive and I would type, then I would drive and he would type. We always insisted on getting rooms in the front of a motel near the office—never in the rear, where you could be dragged out in the middle of the night by the Klan. We used pay telephones because our phones were tapped. One time Claude was on the phone dictating a story when a voice broke in and said, "You nigger-loving son-of-a-bitch!"

Instinctively I recognized this was a great story: It was the good guys against the bad guys, and there was no ambiguity about who was who. I was both fascinated and revolted by it. Every day was a powerful emotional experience.

The first big story I covered was in Albany, Georgia, in 1961. Martin Luther King was there, and every day he would lead a march of 600 or 700 people. The police chief was a very shrewd, very polite guy; he would just put everybody in jail. King learned a lesson from that: You had to have the right enemy. That's why he picked Birmingham as the great battleground. He knew that Public Safety Commissioner Bull Connor would react. So when Connor called out the fire hoses and police dogs, the ensuing spectacle was shared with the nation in *Life* and *Newsweek* magazines. King picked Selma for the same reason. He knew the sheriff there brutally used his mounted posse and dogs, and so he knew what would happen during the confrontation at the Selma bridge. King was, in my view, the first black leader to understand how to use the media.

I had grown up in this macho, "duke it out" white Southern culture: Do not ask for help, and if anybody threatens you, you fight. But King's nonviolence redefined what I thought of as bravery. He and the SNCC [Student Nonviolent Coordinating Committee] kids put themselves in harm's way, but they also cultivated me and Claude because the presence of a *Newsweek* or *New York Times* reporter at a demonstration could lessen the likelihood that they would get jailed, beaten up, or killed.

I completely identified with black people. Some people used to joke with me: "Karl, don't you really wish you were black?" I kind of did, because I wanted to get in the fight. Sometimes I was so sickened by what I saw that I wanted to put down my typewriter and pick up a gun.

*In 1964, Fleming and Sitton covered the kidnapping and murder of three young civil rights workers—Michael Schwerner, Andrew Goodman, and James Chaney—in Philadelphia, Mississippi.*

We drove down to Philadelphia to question the sheriff. He looked very pasty and guilty. He gave us some bullshit story that they had arrested the boys and turned them loose on the edge of town. Claude and I knew immediately that they were dead.

The next morning we came back for another interview. As we were leaving the courthouse, a huge mob of white people backed us into a corner. The leader of the mob said, "If it wasn't for you goddamn nigger-lovin' Jew Communist reporters coming down here and stirring up these niggers, we wouldn't have this trouble. If you don't get your asses out of town, you're going to get killed."

We slipped out the side door of the courthouse and ran across the town square. There was a hardware store owned by a cousin of Turner Catledge—the managing editor of *The New York Times* and Sitton's boss—and we thought we'd be safe there.

Catledge's cousin wasn't all that happy to see us. "Let me tell you how it is," he said. "If you were a couple of niggers and you were down on the ground and this crowd was kicking the crap out of you, I would not take part in that. On the other hand, I wouldn't lift a goddamn finger to help you, either. My advice to you is get your asses out of this town immediately, or you'll be killed."

As we drove off, I told Claude it was a good thing he had so much influence in this town. Otherwise, we'd really be in trouble.

CHAPTER 19

# MOTHER COURAGE

*Carolyn Goodman, mother of Andrew Goodman, one of three young civil rights workers murdered in Mississippi in 1964, lives in the same Upper West Side Manhattan apartment where she and her husband awaited news of his whereabouts. Rather than retreating from the world, though, she became even more active in the fight for civil rights: She created a foundation to encourage youth leadership and multiracial cooperation—and named it for the son who never came home.*

THEY WERE MISSING FOR 44 DAYS. It was horrible because I didn't allow myself to think that they were gone, that they were dead. To me they were missing and that was it, period.

I still have holes in the walls where the FBI put the wires to tap our phone. They were in that back room, and finally some friends said, "Look, you've got to get out of here. You can't stay here and wait for the boys." So finally we went out, to a play or something at Lincoln Center, and while we were there someone came running down the aisle and said, "Come on home. I think they've found them."

What they'd found was the car. Whatever people thought of President Johnson later, he did everything he could. He said, "I want the Marines out. I want the Army out. I want the Navy out. I want to find those boys." He did everything possible—everything.

*On August 4, the FBI, acting on an informant's tip, bulldozed an earthen dam and discovered the three bodies. Goodman and Schwerner had each been shot once in the chest with a .38-caliber revolver; Chaney, his skull fractured, had been savagely beaten and then shot as well. In December, 21 men were arrested for the crime; seven, including Deputy Sheriff Cecil Price, were convicted on federal conspiracy charges in 1967. Price served four years in prison.*

Andy had met the others in Ohio, where he was training with CORE to go down to Mississippi. While they were there, the church in Mississippi where they held the Freedom School meetings was burned to the ground. James and Mickey said, "We've gotta go and see what's going on there. Does anybody want to come with us?" And Andy said, "I'll go."

They drove all night from Ohio. And that's how it happened. They were picked up and put in jail and then they were let out. The Klan was looking for Mickey Schwerner because he was the one who was organizing. And, of course, James was black, and that was the thing that got them so riled up.

I think right after Andy's death there was a passion that I felt, a hurt that you can't live with all the time. It would drown you. But the fact was that he wanted to go south. He stood in our living room and said, "Mom, I gotta go. I just have to go." And I was the one who got his duffel bag and put in bandages and, in those days, iodine and what not. But did I expect him to be killed? Of course not.

My oldest son, Johnny, lived up on 120th Street and he was an extraordinary musician. He had just graduated from NYU's music school, and had been accepted to Julliard for the school of conducting. And when Andy was killed, he just dropped out of everything. All he did was sit in his apartment and watch television. That's all he did. Night and day, watch television.

Then one day he said to me, "You know, something occurred to me —it was like a voice—something said to me, 'Johnny, you can't do this. You're a Jew.' I decided I better find out what it means to be a Jew."

So, even though we weren't a religious family, he decided to go to a local yeshiva. The next thing I know he's wearing a Star of David. He would go to this glatt kosher place on the lower East Side, and meet these Lubavitchers—you know, the ones with the big hats and

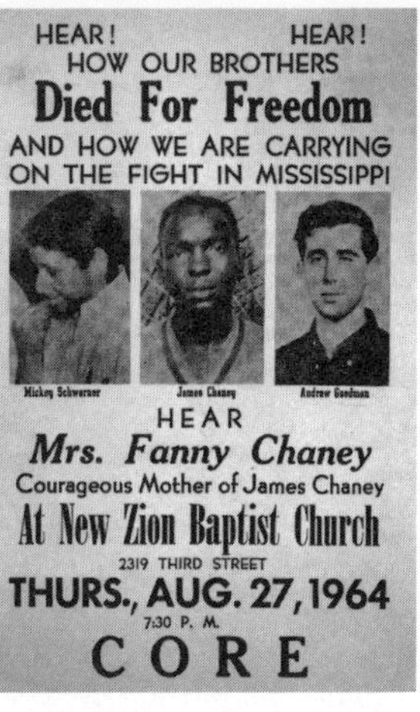


A TORCHED STATION WAGON discovered near Meridian, Mississippi, on June 23, 1964, forebodes the fate of missing civil rights workers Michael Schwerner, James Chaney, and Andrew Goodman. They were found buried beneath an earthen dam 44 days after their disappearance.
Left, Robert and Carolyn Goodman mourn their son.

the beards and what not. One day he came home and said, "Mom, in the Jewish tradition it says in the Bible that I should go to Israel. You go and you multiply." He said, "I think I have to go to Israel." I wasn't happy, but I supported him in the life he had chosen.

My husband, Bobby, always said, "Look, our children know what our values are: We believe in democracy, we believe in freedom, we believe in openness. But we also believe that our children have to select their paths, whatever they are." And you know, they did.

As it turned out, Johnny became religious and Andy chose to go south to help African Americans. The Constitution said everybody should be able to vote, and that's what he believed. He was supposed to go to Canton, Mississippi, and then they switched him. He was not supposed to go to the most dangerous place in the South.

I learned a lot from Andy about the willingness to expose yourself, to really take risks and not know exactly what's going to be the outcome. A few years ago, I spent time in prison for protesting the death of Amadou Diallo [who was shot 19 times by New York City police], and I was no baby then. I can still hear those jail doors bang. I thought, "Oh my God. What am I doing here?" But I was there. Because as long as I got two legs to stand on, I can't be sitting in a corner. It's not my style. And my kids know it. My youngest son, David, said, "Mom, what are you doing out there, for God's sake? Let the kids do it."

We didn't know exactly what to write on Andy's tombstone. Then we heard about a poem Stephen Spender had written in 1933 to honor some antifascists who had been killed by Franco, "I Think Continually of Those Who Were Truly Great." Spender gave us permission to make the pronouns singular rather than plural for Andy's tombstone:

*Born of the sun he traveled a short while towards the sun,*
*And left the vivid air signed with his honor.*

CHAPTER 20

# HOUR OF POWER

*If Dr. Alvin F. Poussaint's name seems familiar, it may be because for eight years the Harvard psychiatry professor moonlighted as a script consultant for* The Cosby Show. *In 1964, as a young doctor fresh out of Harvard Medical School, Poussaint headed south to help provide medical care for civil rights workers and to desegregate health facilities. Along the way, he discovered that many civil rights workers had suffered hidden emotional traumas that could threaten the entire movement.*

A MENACING POLICEMAN stopped me outside my office in Jackson, Mississippi, and said, "What's your name?"

I said, "Dr. Poussaint."

And he said, "What's your *first* name, boy?"

I looked at him and said, "My name's Dr. Poussaint."

My secretary, who was black and from Mississippi, started yanking on my arm. "Tell him your first name," she pleaded.

He put his hand on his gun and said, "What's your first name?"

Finally I said, "Alvin."

He said, "Okay, *Alvin,* next time you give us trouble, we're gonna take you downtown."

Then he spun around and walked away.

I could feel myself starting to tremble. I had thought when he put his hand on his gun that something awful was going to happen. I felt humiliated and terrified.

Later, I felt enraged. I was angry about what he had put me through in order to establish his white superiority over me, no matter who I was.

I was in the South, where there was segregation and black people were "inferior." We don't call you "Doctor" and we don't call you by your last name—you are Alvin, and you are a boy. *And don't you forget it.*

Black people suffered assaults on their dignity every single day, particularly in the South, but in other parts of the country as well. I felt I was fighting back by being in the movement—but sometimes I felt overcome by rage and anger.

I was not alone. I could see the stress in a lot of the other civil rights workers. They would be so stressed out by the combat, by the demonstrations, by being thrown in jail that they didn't know what to do with their enormous inner tension.

Sometimes I would talk to the workers about it. Sometimes I would intercede. One time some black civil rights workers were

WHEN STOKELY CARMICHAEL (shown here at a 1966 rally at the University of California, Berkeley) first shouted his famous "Black Power" slogan, he was "overstressed and mad as hell," says Dr. Alvin Poussaint. "That's why it came across as an angry thing that terrified white people."

released from jail along with some white workers. The two groups had been segregated in jail, and the black kids were enraged while the white kids were just kind of ticked off.

The black workers became angry and started pushing the white kids around. I had to bring the white workers into my office and lock the door so the others couldn't get at them. I understood the black workers' anger—and, incidentally, so did the white workers.

They had all this anger from the humiliation and the abuse they had to suffer. But they couldn't fight back because ours was a nonviolent movement. They also knew it was dangerous—that they would get killed if they fought back.

That was one of the by-products of the movement that I didn't quite understand until I went down there: This anger was all being held inside. Sometimes when workers looked like they were going to break down, we would arrange for them to leave; we'd send them back to their home cities and arrange for some R&R—and, if necessary, psychotherapy.

I was no exception. The incident with the abusive white policeman stayed with me for quite a while. A lot of stuff stayed buried. While I was in Mississippi, I stayed rather calm because I felt I had to be a role model, so I wasn't going to fly off the handle. But the rage was still there. When I got back to Boston after being in Mississippi for two years, I was very withdrawn. I went into therapy. What came out was all this rage and anger. I was also feeling depressed—very fatigued and stressed—and I realized that I'd been using a lot of my energy just to remain functional.

Before I went to Mississippi, I was doing academic studies in psychopharmacology, and I thought I would eventually return to that. But I was such a changed person when I came back to Boston that those studies had no meaning for me anymore. I just didn't care about them. What I cared about now was helping minorities who were disenfranchised. I just had another mission.

I also had to come to grips with the realization that I was haunted by a fear of failure—that I was going to end up like my older brother, who died from an infected needle at age 42. In order to avoid ending up like him and the other guys who overdosed, I had to succeed. Failure meant going back to East Harlem and going down the tubes.

I joined the faculty of Tufts University Medical School, running a psychiatry program in a low-income housing development in Boston.

Like me, a lot of leaders in the movement suffered incredible tension—and like me, they found their stress pushing them in unexpected directions. At one time Stokely Carmichael risked his life because he was under such stress. I remember it very vividly because I helped intervene. In June 1966 we were tear-gassed in Canton, Mississippi, by the police, who ran across the field clobbering everybody, women and children. People were lying on the ground. Little kids were running around thinking they were blind from the tear gas.

Stokely was on the field in a rage at the troopers saying, "You're killing my people! We're not gonna let you!"

He started moving toward the troopers. People said, "Stokely, what are you doing?"

He said, "They're killing my people!"

He had just totally lost it. He was tackled by other workers. We grabbed him and got him over to a car and said, "Take him away. Let him cool out, because he's going to get killed if he goes after these troopers."

He didn't seem to have any control. He was breaking down right there on the field.

The next day, when reporters came to interview him about the tear-gassing, he was still in this rage. Carmichael raised his fist and said, "Black Power! Black Power! Black Power!" It went out all across the country—it was a dramatic moment, a moment that changed America.

That's when the country first began to hear about Black Power. The next week Carmichael was on all these talk shows, and they were running to Roy Wilkins and Whitney Young and Martin Luther King saying, "Explain 'Black Power'!" Roy Wilkins felt that "Black Power" could mean "black death."

But it was forced on the country by that moment in Canton. Carmichael was overstressed and mad as hell. That's why it came across as such an angry thing that terrified white people. They felt the anger in it. He raised his fist and said, "Black Power!" like we're gonna strike back and squash you.

The fact is, people within the movement had been talking about Black Power for some time. If it had emerged as more like a black consciousness thing—evolutionary, developing black pride—it wouldn't have been as scary. But the way Carmichael sounded, everybody, including the FBI, said, "We have to stop these folks." And they began to go after all the Black Power groups.

That's when J. Edgar Hoover put the counterintelligence program in place. He was afraid of Dr. King, but he was also mostly afraid about black revolutionaries being the big threat to the country. He felt the Black Power folk would capture the momentum. That's when Hoover started talking about having to neutralize black leadership.

*Ebony* magazine called me and said, "Will you please give us some insight on what all this 'black consciousness' stuff is about that came out of Mississippi?" I wrote that a big problem for blacks in the movement in Mississippi was that they felt they had internalized racism; they felt inferior. As an example, if white workers in Mississippi called a rally in a black church for 8 p.m., many black people would show up. But if a black organizer called that same rally, few showed up. It was like if a white person was endorsing it, they're powerful and "I'm gonna go."

We had to begin to purge black people of this internalized racism and make them feel black and proud. That's why we switched to the word "black" and took away the word "Negro"—to get away from the negative. "Black" was a derogatory word back then, but we were going to turn that around and make it a positive word. We also felt that blacks had to learn how to organize and do things for themselves because they had been so downtrodden and dependent. The way to do this was to raise their consciousness and make them feel that they could achieve and gain power, that they didn't have to be dependent and disenfranchised.

It was a way of trying to mobilize the black community. And it worked.

CHAPTER 21

# LOVE STORY IN BLACK AND WHITE

*Even in the progressive hotbed of Oakland, California, Constancia "Dinky" Romilly's parents were noted for their activism. Her mother, author Jessica Mitford, worked for the Civil Rights Congress, while her stepfather, Robert E. Treuhaft, was a labor and civil rights lawyer. Yet as Dinky grew up, she rejected her family's contention that racism and segregation are intentional evils perpetrated by white bigots—until the day, that is, when she experienced a shocking awakening of her own.*

MY SENIOR YEAR IN HIGH school I was walking down the hall with several of my white friends, who had decided to have a luncheon at a restaurant. We passed this black girl who was the head cheerleader and I said, "Joyce, do you need a ride to the luncheon?"

I could see she was evading me. Finally she said, "I'm not going."

"What do you mean you're not going? *Everybody's* going."

"Well, I wasn't invited," she said, and walked on.

"What's Joyce talking about?" I said.

One of the girls who had organized the event squirmed and said, "Well, we didn't think she'd be comfortable because everybody that's coming is white."

It was like centuries of ignorance had been stripped away from me. I became hysterical and started physically attacking this girl. I jumped on her, pulled her hair, scratched her. Neither one of us really knew how to fight. Everybody was screaming and people were pulling me off her. She was crying and I was crying.

The white kids were totally embarrassed to have been exposed this way. To have somebody in their own group behave like that was unacceptable.

Even worse, the black kids were just as embarrassed by me: What was I accomplishing? What did I think I was trying to prove? What sort of stupid person was I that I didn't know that this sort of thing went on?

It was like scales had been lifted from my eyes: "Okay," I said, "so my parents are right."

*Romilly had little choice, she recalls, but to bottle up her newfound anguish. She enrolled at Sarah Lawrence College in Bronxville, New York, where she was soon drawn to meetings of the National Student Association. Those in turn exposed her to the leadership of SNCC and a cluster of activists who later formed Students for a Democratic Society (SDS).*

All the militant thinkers were in this group. You can imagine somebody like me, who had just woken up to racism, now having an opportunity to meet others like me, but far more advanced in what they were doing. I had been in the desert, then suddenly this oasis! These people wanted to fight racism. They knew how many thousands of others had not yet realized the American dream.

I didn't know what I wanted to do, yet these people knew what had to be done. They knew that you had to deal with public accommodations, so they staged sit-ins and Freedom Rides. They knew you had to deal with the vote, so they founded the Mississippi Freedom Democratic Party. And they also knew you had to deal with education, so they opened Freedom Schools in Mississippi. [In 1964, over 30 such schools taught more than 3,000 students such fundamental skills as reading, writing, and arithmetic, as well as civil rights and leadership development.]

These people understood that a dynamic movement would be needed to effect social and political change. Not only were they creative—they had ideas about how to do it, which I certainly did not—but they were courageous: The idea of walking into a place where you might get beaten up, or boarding a bus you might get pulled off—well, that was terrifying to me. At the same time, it was the inspiration of a lifetime.

*Romilly worked for the Civil Rights Movement as a Sarah Lawrence student, picketing the Woolworth's in Bronxville, raising funds for SNCC, and helping to organize the first intercollegiate conference on civil rights held in the North.*

Others seemed able to juggle their academic work and their political work, but not me. I just abandoned my course work completely. My parents may have been happy that I was doing political work, but they were not at all pleased I'd "thrown away" my education. We were a very lower-middle-class family. My father, Esmond Romilly, was killed while serving in the Canadian Air Force during World War II, and my mother had saved the money for my college education over the next 17 years. She came from an upper-class English family —her father was the second Baron Redesdale—that had never allowed her to go to school; to them, educating women was a waste of money and time. So she was furious when I got into a university and then just blew it like that.

*Romilly dropped out in her senior year to work full time for the Civil Rights Movement. In 1964 she became SNCC's Northern Coordinator, sending field reports and position papers to supporters around the country.*

I spent every waking moment doing fundraising and publicity for the "Friends of SNCC" in New York. A position paper I wrote for SNCC brought me to the attention of [civil rights leader] James Forman. He came to New York for a Friends of SNCC meeting and said, "Who is Constancia Romilly?"

I said, "I am." He asked me to work for SNCC in Atlanta. Too many useless white people, I thought, were running down to join what was essentially a black movement. Unless you had a skill to contribute, what was the point? I thought we should stay where we were and do whatever we could to support the movement.

And then there was the idea of moving to another city, which was really scary to me. But I went anyway, and it was the fulfillment of a dream I didn't even know I had. To be there and to work with those leaders, to be able to help out in whatever way I could—I discovered a movement that I could not live my life without joining. I knew it was the right thing for me to do.

Working with those black leaders completely changed my life. By watching, observing, reading, I learned things I never could have. I learned about the history and impact of racism from co-workers and colleagues who had experienced it personally. To sit around all night talking to women who'd gone to little country schools, whose families had been in situations like that of Emmett Till, I learned what really happened in the United States vis-à-vis the black population.

I don't like the word "help" because of its occasional connotations of charity or inadequacy. There was nothing this group *couldn't* do.

*In Atlanta, Romilly fell in love with James Forman. The relationship, which subsequently produced two sons, would cause her to leave the SNCC office in Atlanta.*

Jim and I started a romance that was not part of my plan at all. I told myself, "I'm coming here to work—I'm not coming here to have a romantic experience," but you cannot plan when you're going to fall in love with somebody. It happens when you least expect it.

Jim was one of the most charismatic, exciting people. He was an incredibly hard worker, and he could motivate a paper bag. You don't ask somebody else to do something, he believed, that you don't do yourself. He was one of the few people in SNCC with any political education. Most of us had not read political philosophy, which he had, so we didn't know anything in depth about the different forms of organizing a society. Jim taught everybody a lot. At the same time, people resented his control and power.

I didn't want to get involved with anyone working with SNCC because there was too much chatter about white women coming South to hook up with black men. There was a tremendous amount of resentment about Jim and me. Ruby Doris Smith Robinson—this remarkable, amazing woman without whom we couldn't have run that office—opposed my relationship with Jim, who was married when we first started going around together. It was no secret that some of the black women didn't like black-white relationships. They would tell me that black men should hook up with black women, that white women shouldn't come skimming off the leadership and the black men.

My parents were fine with my being involved with a black man, but they were scared for us living as a mixed couple in Atlanta. They worried that the Klan would come around. My father started having nightmares abut that.

When I first met Jim's family, they were uncertain about the idea of Jim being with a white woman. It wasn't seen as the right thing to do. I sort of agreed with them; that had been my position too, and it annoyed me that Jim and I were falling in love.

I told myself, "Let me go someplace where this issue is not quite so front and center, and I'll work there." I really couldn't work in Atlanta anymore, so in 1964 I came back to New York and began working for the Collectors Guild, which sold art lithographs. I also did volunteer work for the Southern Conference Educational Fund (SCEF), which was combating racism and promoting integration. Jim spent a lot of time in New York, doing editorial work and working for SNCC. Our first son was born in 1967.

SNCC had petered out by 1970, largely from lack of funds. After Ruby Doris died of cancer in 1967, nobody knew how to run the organization the same way. Under the leadership of Stokely Carmichael, SNCC allied itself with the Black Panther Party, a move that brought intense government scrutiny. The FBI launched a counterintelligence unit, COINTELPRO, to infiltrate and eviscerate radical black groups.

People were coming around spreading lies about Jim and everybody else. The harassment was constant. I believe someone poisoned Jim in California, and it caused him to have a nervous breakdown. Then he was okay for awhile, but in 1974 he was poisoned again, which I think was accidental. But I decided I couldn't take care of him *and* the two boys. I continued to support him financially as much as I could. He got better, and he became more quiet and peaceful, less radical.

Black Power never coalesced, and the leadership splintered. You had conservative blacks and radical blacks, and once the Civil Rights Movement fell apart there was no possibility of organizing a cohesive force. People were afraid of the Black Panthers, but people in power are always afraid if somebody comes along who wants to take some of that power for themselves. The Panthers didn't start out as an organization that went around shooting people. The shootouts and the violence were responses to harassment and repression.

How many black people have been killed trying to fight for civil rights? A lot. So when blacks suddenly said, "We're not going to sit around and get killed anymore," that must have scared the people who had gotten away with it 'til then.

Egotism was another thing that killed the alliance between SNCC and the Black Panther Party. Respect for the individual in this country, regrettably, often gets twisted into self-aggrandizement and selfishness. Everybody wanted to be top dog; everybody who was a leader was fighting for an edge.

*Romilly's two sons are grown now. James Forman, Jr., is a law-school professor, while Chaka Esmond Forman is an actor. In 1980, Romilly married Terry Weber, a teacher. She got a master's degree in nursing, and in 1998 she set up the Pain Treatment Department at Bellevue Hospital.*

The whole Civil Rights Movement ended legal segregation in the United States, but we didn't put much of a dent in racism. My sons just attended the wedding of a close childhood friend who married a white woman, and the bride's father refused to attend. What's that all about? Our schools are supposedly integrated, but internal segregation persists everywhere.

Our institutions are organized in a very racial way. Housing, for example, is still racially segregated, even though technically that's illegal. Economically, people are still disadvantaged according to the ethnic group they come from. I don't know what will change that; if I knew, I'd be out there organizing. I guess I'm counting on the next generation to pick up the battle flag.

*Yuri Kochiyama, 82, was interned with other Japanese Americans in a camp during World War II. After the war she moved to Harlem, where she met Malcolm X.*

Listening to Malcolm X was like nothing else I had ever experienced. If it wasn't for Malcolm, I would be just another civil rights activist. Malcolm would give the history of when blacks came to this country, through slavery. I had never heard of slavery when I grew up!

I heard him speak often, and once he came to my house for a meeting. I was at the Audubon Ballroom in Harlem when he was assassinated, February 21, 1965. But people felt that Malcolm seemed a little anxious. And then, when it did happen—it was unforgettable. I mean, it was like an explosion.

I followed a guy who was close to the stage. And I got down and put Malcolm's head in my lap. Then his wife, Betty [Shabazz], came in my place. And someone told me to hold the youngest baby, and I went to the room next to the stage, and someone gave me a bottle to give the baby.

People ask me, "What did he say? What were his last words?"

But he was just trying to breathe. He was having a hard time breathing. And then he died.

I hope I said something to him. If I did, I think it would be, "Malcolm, please live, please live."

MALCOLM X

CHAPTER 22

# HARD-WIRED FOR FREEDOM

*Veteran activist Heather Tobis Booth was born in Mississippi in 1945 but moved to Bensonhurst in Brooklyn a year later, thus growing up, as she puts it, in "two places with a history of racial conflict." Drawing on her Jewish heritage, Booth started protesting segregation as a teenager on Long Island. In the years since then she has fought bravely for civil rights, the women's movement, and world peace. The pivotal point in her thinking came after her senior year in high school on a summer trip to Israel.*

I VISITED YAD VASHEM—THE memorial to the Holocaust—and saw thousands of shoes in cases; a room full of hair from people who'd been killed during the Holocaust. The exhibit also told the story of the Warsaw Ghetto. The idea that you have to resist in the face of injustice was deeply affecting.

When I left that museum, I was unable to talk. I came out of there convinced that you just have to struggle for justice in the face of injustice. That's when I decided to come back to the U.S. and work for civil rights. I made a commitment that I *would* fight for justice.

I enrolled at the University of Chicago, and within about two weeks I felt that I had found my home. I got involved in a school boycott challenging the legality of "Willis Wagons." Those were segregated trailer-like facilities that had been thrown up to prevent school integration by stopping protests against unequal education. You would have a black school and then, just a block away, a white school.

You could have integrated them. The black schools were overcrowded and practically falling down, while the white schools had better materials and not just more teachers but more experienced teachers.

Civil rights leaders had called a boycott, and blacks were staying away from the schools in protest, so we set up "Freedom Schools" in churches and community centers. I coordinated the South Side Freedom Schools—finding classroom space and teachers, then making sure the kids were there. The best thing about the experience was the joy of discovering the sense of empowerment that emerges when a community stands up and finds its voice.

*Booth became head of the campus branch of Friends of SNCC and the liaison to the citywide Coordinating Council of Community Organizations. She tutored kids off campus and volunteered in a locked ward at a mental institution.*

The university in those days was invigorating—folk dancing, documentary films, student government—and at the same time a groundswell was rising around the Vietnam war. Civil rights was still my main focus, but I was also waking up to the fact that our values about what society should look like needed to be addressed—and often challenged.

I was coming back to the campus late one night in 1964 because a friend of mine had threatened suicide. I sat up with him until all hours, and when I returned I got a reprimand because I had broken the parietal hours [restrictions on when members of the opposite sex can visit a campus dormitory]. They also searched me for contraceptives! I was outraged. For me, the episode became a personal immersion in women's issues, since men did not have these schedule restrictions.

We organized a group that stayed out later at night. Then a friend of mine was raped in her bed in off-campus housing. When she went to Student Health for an exam, they lectured her about "promiscuity" and claimed that Student Health did not cover gynecological exams. So we sat with her because she was in need, and it became a sit-in. We weren't going to leave until she got an exam.

In 1964 I volunteered to be a voter registrar and a Freedom School teacher in Mississippi's "Freedom Summer." I was one of the youngest volunteers—still barely 18 years old. It was clearly a transforming experience for me. We were trained in nonviolence so you wouldn't react when you were insulted or intimidated. We were confronted by the realities of being blacks and whites in real proximity, with real conflicts. We were challenged about the role of whites in a racist society. You couldn't figure out a new arrangement—you couldn't create a "beloved community"—until tensions from the past had been understood and appreciated.

Being so young, I mostly remember being scared, but also impressed by the courage and generosity of the people fighting for justice in Mississippi. In the town of Shaw, for example, there was a lot of intimidation. One night a bomb threat was called in. We were at the Freedom School and told to lie on the floor in the dark. Cars and trucks were driving around, flashing their lights, honking and making noises. We had an open line to the Jackson office of CORE just in

FLEDGLING ACTIVIST Heather Tobis Booth entertains Fannie Lou Hamer, a former sharecropper who turned into a fiery civil rights leader.

COATED WITH KETCHUP and beaten, Professor John R. Salter sits tall at a 1963 lunch-counter protest in Jackson, Mississippi. To his left sit comrades Joan Trunpauer and Anne Moody. Two months later in Cambridge, Maryland *(below)*, police drag three demonstrators off to jail.

case. They gave up, but it was still intimidating, and I had to wonder what life was like for people who lived there all the time.

I lived with the Hawkins family. Andrew Hawkins was a leader in the Mississippi Freedom Democratic Party (MFDP). The Democratic Party there was so racist it wouldn't allow black participation, so the MFDP was set up as an alternative. The MFDP had its own registration and its own delegates; they traveled to the national convention in Atlantic City, but the mainstream Democratic Party refused to seat them.

Andrew Hawkins knew more than I did about everything related to current events. He was getting the *Chicago Defender* regularly. His family was generous with their house, their food, their time, their education, and their tolerance of us. When they showed us the bed where four of us would sleep, I realized, "This is Mr. and Mrs. Hawkins' bed." I have no idea where they slept. Plus they had five kids.

It was a cultural experience of eye-opening dimensions, both on rural poverty and on how another part of America lives. They had a rambling wood house with a little porch and an outhouse. The pig they owned would wander in and out, and there were chiggers in the bed. I got chiggers up and down my legs, and the only way to get them off was with gasoline. But this was how the Hawkins family lived every day.

Part of our purpose was to register people to vote. But the local officials did not want black people to vote, because they would be voting to change the way things were. First we'd take people to the official voter-registration office, which was always closed down. Then we went on Freedom Registration drives, asking people to register for the Freedom Democratic Party. We would go to remote rural areas and ask people if they would sign a voter registration form. We must have scared people out of their minds—imagine a white girl just showing up at your farmhouse—but many people signed. They were willing to take a risk for freedom and the future.

*When civil rights workers Andrew Goodman, Michael Schwerner, and James Chaney were reported missing and later found murdered, Booth's normally supportive parents grew distraught.*

My mother could not talk on the phone. She could only cry. My father, who had been so loving to me growing up, was yelling into the phone about how I was killing my mother. I was living the values they had, but their fear divided us for a time. And what could the fear be like for those African Americans who lived their lives in Mississippi?

When I got back to Chicago, I did not know how to deal with my culture shock. How do you convey what it's like to live under threat and tyranny all the time, and to act in spite of it? To live in poverty and act out of generosity? To be part of something—building a better society for your kids—you're willing to risk your life for?

*Back on campus, Booth heard about a friend who needed an abortion. The experience of locating medical care for her moved Booth to establish a counseling service, which had facilitated 11,000 abortions by the time* Roe v. Wade *overturned the anti-abortion law in 1973. The service, called Jane, has been the subject of a book, a play, and a movie.*

Not surprisingly, tensions were percolating over the roles of men and women in both the Civil Rights and antiwar movements. By now I was a fairly experienced speaker, and I was talking at an SDS [Students for a Democratic Society] meeting in 1965 when this guy got up and told me to shut up. I tapped the shoulder of every woman in the group and said, "Let's go upstairs," and we left. We formed a group called WRAP, for Women's Radical Action Project. I'm now told it was one of the first campus women's organizations in the country.

At a winter SDS conference in Champaign-Urbana, we had explored "the woman question," as it was called. After the conference I wrote a paper asking why women held only certain positions within the SDS. From that it became clear that the men didn't want to let the women talk; they were denying the women's reality.

Jimmy Garrett had gotten up at the SDS conference and said, "You [women] are not going to get this together unless you go off by yourselves." He was probably drawing from the history of the Civil Rights Movement. There are reasons to organize together, but there are also reasons to organize around their particular interests. Initially I thought, "Oh no, let's all just talk together. We can figure this out." But after a few hours I realized that was not going to happen. I went off with some women and we agreed to set up women's groups.

*Heather met Paul Booth, the SDS national secretary, at a sit-in to protest the university's cooperation with the Selective Service. "Three days later he asked me to marry him," she recalls, "and five days later I said yes. We got married a year later." Paul and Heather's son Gene was born in 1968. A second son, Dan, followed in 1969.*

*When Dr. King's assassination triggered the April Riots of 1968, Heather Booth—by now a teacher at a special high school for dropouts—faced "aiding and abetting" charges for allowing her students to discuss the events. Her teaching job ended after she took maternity leave for her second son. An editorial job was terminated when she fought for fellow workers whose pay had been cut. Booth sued and won, and the settlement enabled her to start the Midwest Academy in 1973. Still going strong today, the academy teaches people how to build grassroots citizen organizations.*

*The couple moved east when Paul was called to Washington, D.C., in 1998 to work for the American Federation of State, County, and Municipal Employees (AFSCME). With her training system emerging as a national model, and with her political experience, Booth was appointed by the Democratic National Committee to set up a template for political training activities. Later she began international organizing work, aiding Nigeria's first democratic election in 1998.*

The call from Julian Bond at the NAACP came in 2000, asking me to direct a new organization called the NAACP National Voter Fund. This was the largest African American voter mobilization in history. It helped increase African American voter turnout by two million.

My drive to change the world must be hard-wired into me. When I was in high school and had moved out of Brooklyn, my first-grade teacher, Mrs. Greenhouse, tracked me down and came to our house to tell this story. I didn't remember it, but I was really touched that she had taken the trouble.

There was one African American boy in my class in first grade; his name was Benjamin, and he was my friend. Apparently Benjamin was being taunted by the other kids, who had formed a circle around him. I walked through the circle, stood next to him, and put my arm around him.

We're all in this together.

CHAPTER 23

# HELP FROM ON HIGH

*In 1966 Curtis Graves broke the color barrier in the Texas Legislature, along with future U.S. Congresswoman Barbara Jordan. Now 65 and living in Tucker, Georgia, Graves leaned over his dining room table and related the lessons he learned from his mother and father—and the moment he realized that the cause of liberty was more important to him than life itself.*

I NEVER WILL FORGET MY DAD pulling up to a hole in the ground in New Orleans where some people were digging. "Son, you see what's in that man's hand?"

And I said, "Yes, a shovel."

"That's not a shovel," he said. "It's an ignorant stick." Then he said, "If you don't stay in school and do something with your life, you will work the ignorant stick with that man."

I never forgot that, because that's what you do if you don't have an education. He was pushing me all along.

My mom was the reason I never felt any different from anybody else. I can remember just like it happened yesterday. We'd go to the segregated theater and I'd say, "Why can't we sit downstairs?"

She'd say, "Because you can see better from up here." No matter what, she always had an explanation.

But one Friday night she realized she could tell me the truth. The lights came on after the movie was over, and I looked downstairs and I said, "Mother, I know why we're not downstairs."

And she said, "Why?"

"Because we're not white."

Walking back from the movie that night, she told me what segregation was. Before that, my parents didn't want to deal with it, because they didn't want me to feel any different from anybody else.

When I got to Texas Southern University, the sit-ins had started around the country and we were electrified. Those of us who cared were upset that in Houston, nothing had happened (Houston was a pretty racist town). A few of us got together and decided to march down to Weingarten's, a supermarket with a lunch counter that served only whites. We did it, 12 of us. We sat in and closed the lunch counter down. That was in my junior year, 1960.

Nobody got arrested that first time—not like in a lot of other cities. We had called the police department and the press in advance, because we thought that would be our protection. The police were there but nothing happened.

Twelve of us had started that little movement, but by the next Saturday we had 200 people. By the third Saturday, we had thousands. It just caught on like wildfire. We had two things going for us: Houston's business community did not want a black eye—they did not want any violence—and the entire TSU campus was mobilized. We had access to 3,000 or 4,000 kids, as well as to doctors, lawyers, and other professionals in town.

On the third weekend we faced real trouble. Some skinheads had come in from Galveston on motorcycles to stop the "niggers." We're sitting at the lunch counter at Madding's Drug Store on a Saturday morning, looking into these huge mirrors, when we see these thugs walk in. Just then, in walks a police captain wearing a white hat. He zigzags his way between the skinheads and us, then backs the skinheads up without saying a word.

I kept talking to the kid next to me: "Don't move, keep looking forward, and keep your books in front of you."

To myself, I said, "Well, following Dr. King, I'm not going to fight. I know I'm going to get stabbed and die right here. This is the end." But the skinheads walked out, got on their motorcycles, and drove off. In that brief moment, I had resolved to myself that I was willing to die for the cause.

Later we learned an interesting thing about the Houston sit-ins. TSU Board of Regents chairman Mack Hannah [who was also a prominent businessman], college president Dr. Samuel Nabrit, Governor Allan Shivers, and the police had allowed the protests to play out peacefully because they figured it would give them a bad name if the city exploded. None of us student demonstrators knew this was happening, and I was astonished to find out what they were orchestrating behind our backs. But it showed foresight. When you think of Birmingham or Selma, what it conjures up in your mind is always negative. You don't get that when you think of Houston.

We went home that summer and came back with more things to be done, like hotels and jobs, but the mayor put together a biracial committee and succeeded in putting a lid on the whole thing. We didn't know what to do.

Through Andrew Young, who'd been my friend for years—he was on Dr. King's staff—we got to Dr. King. I explained to him that the biracial committee was actually a sellout group trying to stop our demonstrations, and that we needed some national leadership to help us organize. He listened and listened and then said, "I'll tell God about it."

It blew me away. When somebody tells you that, you don't know what to say. Essentially he prayed about it and—I don't know how to explain this—within three days the biracial committee was dissolved and things continued as planned.

In October 1967, when I was in the state legislature, Andy Young called and said the Southern Christian Leadership Conference needed to raise money for the Poor People's Campaign. I put together a fundraiser. We got Aretha Franklin, Joan Baez, and Harry Belafonte to come for a big concert.

Everything's in place when suddenly the ticket agency gets a bomb threat and pulls out. The event was on a Saturday, and Martin Luther King came in the Friday before. We hadn't sold 500 tickets, and the auditorium seated 3,000 or 4,000. I met King in his suite at the Shamrock Hilton Hotel and said, "We're not going to have but a handful of people in this big auditorium. We're going to look bad."

"Just a moment," he said. Then he stood up, turned around, faced the chair that he was sitting on, knelt, and started talking out loud to

God. He talked for 15 or 20 minutes. Harry Belafonte and I and a couple of other guys in the room were kind of rolling our eyes. When he was done, King stood up, turned around, sat down, and said, "Give away the tickets."

Working out of a friend's garage (we couldn't get anybody to handle the tickets for us), we started planning ways to give away the tickets at supermarkets. A limousine pulled up and a black guy got out with a chauffeur's cap on. He walked up and said, "Who's in charge?" A guy pointed at me. The chauffeur said, "My boss sent me here with a contribution for your show."

"How much?" I asked.

"Ten thousand dollars," he said. "And he doesn't want any tickets. Give them away."

Now, I'm not saying there's a connection between Martin's prayers and this development, but I'm saying that's what happened.

When I learned that Dr. King had been killed, I was sitting down writing a speech in my apartment in Houston. The phone rings and it's a rabbi friend, Moishe Kahna.

"Is your television on?" he asked.

"No."

"Turn it on," he said. "I'm calling because of your friend, Martin King. He has been shot. I was with him last Sunday, and he'd asked me to give you his love."

I broke down, crying. I tried to keep a speaking engagement that night, but started crying and had to walk off the stage. The next day I was driving to San Antonio, and for the first time in my life I saw all the bluebonnets in bloom. It was a spiritual experience. By the time I got to San Antonio, I was a more mature person than the man who had left Houston that morning. I was blessed to have known King, but I had decided that now it was time to move on.

THE DAY BEFORE his assassination, Martin Luther King, Jr., stands on the balcony of the Lorraine Motel in Memphis with *(from left)* Hosea Williams, Jesse Jackson, and Ralph Abernathy. The next day—April 4, 1968—King supporters point out where the gunshots came from.

CHAPTER 24

# AT HISTORY'S ELBOW

*He devoted his life to helping tear down the walls of segregation, but the Rev. Samuel Billy Kyles is probably best remembered for the moment he wishes never happened: On April 4, 1968, he was standing beside Dr. Martin Luther King, Jr., on the balcony of the Lorraine Motel in Memphis just moments before a sniper's bullet cut down the civil rights leader.*

WHEN THE MOVEMENT STARTED in the South, I said, "I need to be a part of this. This is going to be something." At the time, I was an assistant pastor of Tabernacle Baptist Church in Chicago, and had a wife and three kids. I started going to Memphis as a visiting preacher. I'd take the train down there for $10 a week, two Sundays a month, to preach at the Monumental church.

All my friends said, "You're crazy. You're in Chicago, the 'Promised Land.' Why are you going to Egypt voluntarily?"

But I saw it as a grand opportunity to do what I wanted to do.

I got involved with the NAACP in Memphis. One Saturday night there was a big civil rights rally and somebody said, "Monday morning 500 black preachers are going to ride the bus and go to jail! Can you imagine what this town would be like if 500 black pastors were in jail?" And the place went wild.

But Monday morning came and there weren't 500 preachers; there weren't even five preachers. There were just two: me and Dr.

Jim Netters, who still pastors at Mt. Vernon Baptist Church. I call him my jail buddy.

We got on a bus with five other protesters. When I took a seat in the front, the driver stopped the bus and told me to go to the back. I didn't move.

He said, "You know I'm going to have to call the police."

I said, "Do what you have to do."

While we were waiting for the police to come, the other black people on the bus said, "Reverend, why don't you come on back here where you belong so we can go to work?" I went in the back, and I had a little civil rights meeting in the back of the bus.

I said, "Let me ask you something: Do you see a steering wheel back here?"

They said, "No."

I said. "How can we ever drive the bus if the steering wheel is up front and we can't sit there? Our tax money helps support the bus system, and we can't ride up front. Does that make sense?"

They said, "Yeah, Reverend, we'll wait."

My heart jumped. There was definitely a change of heart, a change of mind.

I have been blessed to be involved in integrating the schools. My five-year-old daughter, Dwania, was one of 13 children to integrate the schools in Memphis in the late 1960s. When I lecture around the country, I tell young people, "I took my daughter, Dwania, to school in Memphis, Tennessee, under police protection. This was not in Zimbabwe, not in South Africa, but in Memphis, Tennessee, U.S.A."

That first morning, the police came to my house to escort us to school and protect us from the howling mob. When we got to the school, the police had it surrounded. No howling mob—the police were the mob.

I got out of the car with my daughter. The two plainclothes policemen who had come to escort us introduced me to the police officer in charge at the school. I said, "Good morning, how are you?" and stuck out my hand. He looked at me as if I had leprosy. He never touched my hand.

As we walked up the sidewalk lined with police, the cops said the nastiest things: "Why don't you get that black bitch out of here? Why don't you niggers stay in your place?"

Teachers smelled her hair, rubbed her skin like she was a thing. She wouldn't talk about it. I'd ask her what happened in school and she would just say, "Oh, nothing." But later she'd get to talking to her younger sister and it would all come out.

The incident that affected her most happened much later, when she got the lead role in the school play at Central High. The male lead was white. The kids had no problem with that. But the teacher canceled the play, saying she would not have any interracial casting on her watch.

My daughter just cried and cried. She said, "Daddy, I am sick of this mess. I want to go to a black college."

I said, "That's fine. You can go to a black college, but when you get out the world will still be diverse, and you've got to live in it." So she went to Spelman College in Atlanta, then transferred to Howard University in Washington, D.C., and graduated from there.

At about a quarter of six in the evening I was up on the balcony of the motel with Martin. He was in a playful mood, saying hello to people down in the courtyard. Martin was leaning over the rail talking to Jesse Jackson, who was down in the courtyard with bandleader Ben Branch from Memphis.

I said, "Come on, guys, let's go," and had just stepped off the balcony when a shot rang out. People were ducking. I looked back and saw that Martin had been knocked from the railing back on the balcony. I rushed to his side, and there was this tremendous hole in the side of his neck. I ran to call an ambulance, but I couldn't get anybody on the phone. The motel's operator had left the switchboard when she heard the shot and gone out into the courtyard. When she realized that Martin had been shot, she collapsed in the courtyard with a heart attack. She died the next day.

I ran back out and the police were coming with their guns drawn.

"Call an ambulance on your police radio!" I hollered. "Dr. King's been shot!"

They said: "Where did the shot come from?" That's when the famous picture of the people pointing on the balcony was taken.

I took one of the bedspreads and I covered him from his neck down. There was blood everywhere. The assassin had used dumdum bullets—the ones that mushroom—so there was a big hole in his chest, and he was bleeding profusely. It was a nightmare. There's no way to describe how I felt, to be standing that close to a friend one moment and the next he's gone.

I asked myself, "Why was I there?" It took me a long time to figure that out, but eventually it became clear to me that I was there to be an independent witness who must tell the truth. Martin Luther King, Jr., didn't die in some untoward way, some foolish way. With all his talent and training, he died on a balcony in Memphis, Tennessee, helping garbage workers, poor folks.

I tore up my schedule so I could spend my time talking to people about Martin and what I saw that day—because it has to be told.

JUMPING FOR JOY,
a girl celebrates Nelson Mandela's
election as President of
South Africa on April 27, 1994.

# III

## THE WINGS OF THE FUTURE

*"The future is another word for the soul."*

**Jacob Needleman**

CHAPTER 25

# FOUNDING SISTERS

*Susan Brownmiller is best known for her landmark book about rape,* Against Our Will. *Feminists worldwide are still reaping the benefits of the lessons she learned as a young civil rights worker one summer in Mississippi.*

I WAS BORN IN BROOKLYN IN 1935. My mother was a secretary, my father a not-terribly-successful salesman. My parents were Roosevelt Democrats. I always had a radical streak, but I was not a "red-diaper baby."

Recently I was watching a documentary about the John F. Kennedy years. When Kennedy gained the presidency, it never occurred to him that civil rights would be on his agenda. What made him think about it? A movement of people put it on his agenda.

Change in this country comes from people's movements. It doesn't come from electoral politics or legislation. It starts with very special people who declare themselves soldiers in an unpaid volunteer army of the moral, knowing they can really make change.

Black Southern students got it done. The passage of the civil rights bill had nothing to do with what Kennedy or Johnson felt morally. It was in response to pressure. The same was true for the women's movement. Nobody was going to make things easier for women until we had a movement.

When I first got to Mississippi in 1964, I felt really good. White folks in Meridian looked surprised to see me walking down the street with a black woman or a black man; with our leaflets and our little folders tucked under our arms, we were so clearly civil rights workers. "You don't look like them at all!" a woman told me on the street. "You're not dirty!"

I didn't take jeans to Mississippi. The typical image of a civil rights worker was that of a beatnik, so I dressed in conservative clothes—long skirts and flowered blouses. I was determined that the local whites would look at me and see someone who looked just like them. And I did. I got the look down right.

After Freedom Summer, the movement changed. Everybody was exhausted. Bob Moses apparently felt the weight of the deaths of the three workers, Chaney, Schwerner, and Goodman. He took it hard that he had initiated a project in which people died. That fall, he opted out of the movement. The rest of the people—the black and white workers who had been there for a couple of years—were burned out. SNCC sorely missed his leadership, and it went through this very intense phase of looking at itself. People were asking, "Who are we?"

Some of the older workers said, "What do you mean, 'Who are you?' Ask the FBI, they'll tell you who you are."

I was a lowly white volunteer, sitting in by chance at the famous SNCC conference held in Waveland, Mississippi, to discuss the organization's future. The stars were there—Stokely Carmichael, Ella Baker, Bob Moses—but when they noticed me and my white friend sitting there, they said, "Excuse me, would you two leave?" They ejected us.

Some other whites there were allowed to remain. The gesture was mortifying and infuriating, but at that time I didn't see it as the ejection of whites. In fact, just such a move was under discussion at Waveland. They certainly didn't want us, as strangers with no credentials as far as they were concerned, listening to them deliberate about it.

Eventually, whites were expelled from SNCC. Some of them cried and protested about how long they'd been there, but by this time H. Rap Brown was in charge of SNCC, and there was no room for whites and that concept of the "beloved community." There was no room for a white volunteer standing arm in arm with a black volunteer. Whites had been part of that early and wonderful phase of the movement, but the lines hardened as input came from the northern ghettos.

All movements run on a certain kind of sexual energy, and there were a lot of interracial affairs in the Civil Rights Movement. You're spending day and night with this group of people, and it's quite natural to find a loved object within that group. It just happens. It was particularly poignant and emotional in the Civil Rights Movement because you were breaking that old [racial] barrier. But it was also in the heat of the struggle. It was incredibly romantic.

As several white women and men discovered, however, what worked in Mississippi did not work up North. What may have seemed wonderful in the crucible of the South and all of that political activity became a problem when you had to face up to the reality of life outside that crucible. And perhaps you weren't really suited for each other after all. Relationships broke up for a variety of reasons. I really wish somebody would write about that aspect of the Civil Rights Movement—how human beings find each other under extraordinary circumstances—but it would probably have to be done as a novel.

*Feeling there was nothing much left for white volunteers to do, the 30-year-old Brownmiller left Mississippi for a reporting job at a Philadelphia television station. Later she became a news writer at ABC-TV, then left that post in 1968 to work as a magazine writer.*

*It was not long before Brownmiller segued from covering the Women's Movement to catalyzing it.*

My friend Jan Goodman, who had gone to Mississippi with me, kept telling me that women were meeting in New York. "I don't believe it," I said. I didn't want to go, because in my mind my organizing days were over. But I went to one meeting and that led to another, and by 1969 I was a full-time feminist activist.

The Women's Movement, especially the radical wing, was exceptionally creative in conceptualizing new political issues—starting with abortion—that had never been thought of as political issues in this country. The Women's Movement was founded on the model of the Civil Rights Movement; it borrowed a lot of its techniques, notably the sit-in, which was incredibly effective: Just a small group of dedicated people was all it took to get a whole lot of press attention.

FEMINIST LEADERS confer in 1972. From left, they are *Ms.* magazine editor Gloria Steinem, lawyer Brenda Feigen Fasteau, National Organization of Women president Wilma Scott Heide, and author Betty Friedan.

In March 1970, I organized a sit-in of 200 women at *The Ladies' Home Journal.* I took it straight from the civil rights sit-ins, but with the understanding that it had to be done more irreverently, because we were women sitting in at a glossy magazine office in New York City. Some people thought the cops would drag us away, but 11 hours later the editors settled with us, agreeing to let us publish eight pages—unedited!—in their magazine. John Mack Carter, the *Journal's* editor at the time, later told me that day had changed his life. From that point on, he never failed to mention the Women's Movement and that historic sit-in—which Carter called "the most interesting and transformative day" of his career.

We had organized it exquisitely, tipping off all the major media outlets in advance. We marched in at 9:15, just after the staff had all arrived, and found our way to Carter's office. Fifteen minutes later, Marlene Sanders from ABC-TV News came in with her film crew. By then the word had gone out on the AP wire as well. Marlene thrust her microphone under Carter's nose and said, "So, what do you think of what these women are doing?" And Carter could not speak. He lost his voice for many hours. He just sat there numb. He was a sophisticated man, but he had never expected a sit-in in his office.

Another technique was consciousness raising—using "speaking out" to publicize our experiences with being able, or unable, to get an abortion. In the South, the church was a safe place, and blacks could meet there to strategize; it was a haven where they could testify about how they had tried to vote but couldn't. They would practice nonviolent techniques of protecting their bodies, so that if they were hit they could shield their heads, private organs, and faces.

The Women's Movement had a lot to do with biology—the long history of women's roles and the sexual nature of the discouragement used against us: "No, you can't have an abortion." This wasn't a case of blatant segregation or discrimination, white to black. So while we adopted techniques from the Civil Rights Movement, our issues were trickier.

*In* Against Our Will, *Brownmiller contended that rape is to women what lynching was to blacks—a conscious process of intimidation. Angela Davis and Kathleen Cleaver, among other black radicals, excoriated Brownmiller for the analogy.*

We were raising issues that weren't on the black radicals' agenda. We were making comparisons they found odious. I never renounced my stance, but I was hurt and angry that Angela Davis never let up on it.

The lynching of black men (and some women) in the South made all black people afraid. Everyone knew it could happen if they stepped out of line. Rape plays the same role in the lives of women. Whether they can articulate it or not, they know that if they step out of line—if they climb a mountain without a couple of male buddies, if they hitchhike, if they walk down a street late at night—rape is a specific danger.

Central both to lynching and to rape was the concept of the white woman as the white man's property. The criticism that I was a racist was exceedingly painful; it remains so today. I felt that I had led an exemplary life—far more so than the younger white women who were also calling me a racist. I had spent the early part of the '60s working for civil rights.

We needed to build bridges, yet the early Women's Movement did not really attract black women. White women started to get up at meetings and say, "I won't go to another meeting unless everyone brings at least one black woman."

Our issues were every woman's issues, but for black women to carry two movements was too much of a burden; they felt the Women's Movement was a distraction from the goal of full equality for blacks. I felt that our issues were the right ones. If what we were saying triumphed, *everyone* would benefit.

Being called a racist was not the only thing that angered me. I was also attacked by the lesbians in the Women's Movement. When some of us tried to talk about men at certain meetings, women would stomp their feet and clap their hands. "Forget men," they said. "Come out of the closet."

"Well, I can't," I said. "I'm sorry, but I'm not a lesbian."

Ultimately, the attacks over the years made it easier for me to leave the movement. I took a lot of fire because I said things that didn't follow a politically correct position. The racist charges hurt me more than the homophobic charges, but there were more lesbians in the Women's Movement than there were blacks. So I was confronted more by the homophobia.

Do I miss the Women's Movement? I don't miss going to the meetings and having the fights. I don't ever want to do that again. But I do miss a time when our ideas were central to the thinking in this country. At one time we had the ears of the nation; they were listening, and it was exciting to be one of the voices they heard.

Nobody could have predicted before February 1, 1960 [the date of the pathbreaking Woolworth lunch counter sit-in in Greensboro, North Carolina], that an indigenous Civil Rights Movement would start in the South and transform the face of America. Nobody could have predicted that a Women's Movement would emerge within that same decade.

At some point in the future, a new period of militants will arise. I hope I'm around to see it. If there was a radical older person's movement, I'd join it—put my jeans back on again and sit in at the Medicare office.

CHAPTER 26

# UNPRINCIPLED PRINCIPAL

*Never mind the ready laughter: José Angel Gutiérrez, 59, is all business when it comes to organizing Mexican American political groups, representing Hispanic clients in court, or teaching political science at the University of Texas in Arlington. Racism, he has learned in a 35-year career as a local politician and militant activist, can attack from any direction—even from those we respect the most.*

MY HIGH SCHOOL PRINCIPAL was my hero. He was an Anglo fellow by the name of John B. Lair, an ex-Marine, about six-two, burly guy, tough. I was convinced that I was going to grow up to be just like him—you know, that big. I wanted to be a Marine. He was what I thought a man ought to be. My dad had died when I was 12, so I was looking for this father image. I put this guy in my father's place.

In my junior year, when I was 16, I was elected the school's first Chicano class president. It was the first year there had been more Mexicans than Anglos in the class. The Anglos block-voted, so I got the Mexicans to nominate me but not anybody else.

The main duty of the junior class president was to stage the prom for the seniors and run the election of prom servers from the sophomore class. They served in pairs—one boy and one girl—greeting the seniors as they came into the prom, bringing food and punch to the tables. It was a big deal. So we held the election for prom servers, and I took the results to Principal Lair.

I had my little paper bag with the ballots, and a sheet showing the results. He looked at them. Because the students had not elected an equal number of Mexican and Anglo boys and girls, some of the Anglo boys were matched with Mexican girls, and some of the Mexican boys with Anglo girls.

The principal took my bag of ballots and put it in the trash. He took my little sheet of paper with the prom servers' names on it, tore it up, and put that in the trash too. Then he opened his drawer, pulled out a fresh sheet of paper, and drew a line down the middle. Finally, he wrote down a list of names to please himself—not the names of the people we had elected. Mexican names were on one side, Anglos on the other.

"This is who we're going to have," he said. "We're not going to have any race mixing here."

"But that's not right," I said. "That's not what happened in the election."

He said, "Well, that's the way it's going to be."

"It's still not right," I said. "I'm going to call the media and I'm going to—"

"You do that," he said, "and you're going to be suspended."

At that moment, I realized I had no power. Everything they told us in class about the ideals of voting and fairness and all that was bullshit in practice.

I couldn't even talk, you know. That really crushed me.

In a moment, my hero became my enemy. And I vowed, "I'm going to get this guy one day."

As a little kid, you're not aware. You see things as normal because that's what everybody is subjected to. Even at the movies, I didn't realize we were segregated. I just thought it was cool to sit in the balcony.

Because of my father and mother, I had to be a real Mexican at home. I had to adhere to the culture—all the values and mores of being a Mexican. That meant speaking Spanish properly, discussing things in Spanish, following the customs.

The whole point of public schools was to make Anglos out of all of us. But out on the street when the bell rang, Anglos went one way and we went the other.

So we had to learn to be three different people in different situations. We were Mexicans mostly at home, and Anglos mostly at school. Out on the streets, though, you had to be a Chicano—an American of Mexican ancestry—with an attitude. On the street I was trying to be something that I couldn't be at home, and at home I was trying to be what I couldn't be outside. The Mexicans didn't like us and the Anglos didn't like us. We had to learn to like ourselves.

In high school I got involved in debate and public speaking. I was very good, so I won some championships, but when we went to travel they would put me in a segregated room. I was told, "It's because you're special, you're the champ. You get a room by yourself."

I told one girl, "I've got this room because I'm so good!"

She said, "You dumb shit, you get this room because you're the Mexican."

You know, all of these things began to mesh. And I began to see. The Anglos' streets are paved. Our streets are not paved. There are sidewalks over there. No sidewalks over here. Then you wonder, why are all the Mexicans in vocational or non-college-preparatory classes? None on the varsity football team. The football sweetheart, why is she white? Why is there only one Mexican cheerleader? You really begin to realize all those things.

About a month after my run-in with the principal over the election, we had Activities Night—the program where they announce the most handsome, the most beautiful, the most popular, the most this, the most that. It was a big deal in high school. We had an assembly, and they would announce all these.

To pick the winners, we'd sent pictures of the candidates to Troy Donahue and Kim Novak. And, you know, we didn't hear a thing from them.

The event was getting closer and closer—and one day, on the journalism teacher's desk, I found two packages from Hollywood. One was from Kim Novak and the other was from Troy Donahue. Both letters said something like, "We really can't be judges of your beauty. You've got all these beautiful kids."

Well, within three days, the school announced that they had

gotten letters from Kim Novak and Troy Donahue. And I'll be goldanged if they didn't pick kids who were all Anglos.

I realized these people don't want us to get anything. And they'll cheat, they'll lie, they'll do whatever. That taught me they were up to no good, and that you had to watch every move they made. Everything was a trick. They just did not see us as equal.

In 1971 I was elected school board chairman on the Raza Unida Party ticket—and suddenly I was the boss of my old principal, Mr. Lair. The new school board held a meeting to explain how things were going to be from now on. We told him we were going to have bilingual and bicultural education.

"You mean I've got to learn Spanish?" he asked.

"Yes," I told him. "But you've got three years to do it in."

We wanted to have Chicano studies in the curriculum. We also told him we were not going to have any more military recruiters in the schools, because we didn't want any more Chicanos to go over to Vietnam and get killed.

A few weeks later, Mr. Lair died from a heart attack.

*He lives in Chicago now, but the lilting twang proves there's still a lot of Texan in Juan Andrade, who runs the 22-year-old United States Hispanic Leadership Institute. Andrade learned the power of leadership more than 40 years ago from the images flickering across a television screen glimpsed through a neighbor's screen door.*

Whites didn't tell us we couldn't vote—they just said it's going to cost you $1.75. A poll tax. Blacks couldn't afford it, and neither could we. Low-income whites couldn't either. People wouldn't pay $1.75 to register to vote today, let alone in the '50s and '60s. We were a family of seven and our grocery bill for the week was under $20. You could feed a family for almost half a week on what it would cost to register those in our family old enough to vote.

If you wanted to vote, you had to register a year ahead of time. Who in the hell pays attention to races, or issues, a year ahead of time?

They didn't say we couldn't vote—they just said we had to pass a literacy test in English. In Crystal City, Texas, where I briefly taught school, Mexicans made up 90 percent of the county's population. The average education was two years of school. Who in the hell could pass a literacy test?

They weren't telling us we couldn't vote—they just told us we had to own property first. Hell, I was the last of five kids. My parents had no home of their own until I was born; up 'til then, they had rented rooms from other families. My father said, "My last baby is going to be born in his own home." So he bought one for a little under $400.

We didn't get our first television until 1960. Before that we went to a neighbor's house to watch through the windows and screen doors. My father and I watched the Democratic National Convention when John Kennedy was nominated—that was a whole new thing for us. After that, we started seeing Martin Luther King and the Civil Rights Movement. Putting that struggle in front of America's face on the nightly news, that had to embolden everyone who suffered from discrimination, oppression, or injustice.

We were farm workers. Like everybody else, we improvised. We had dirt streets and outdoor toilets. We played ball in the streets. In the public schools they would punish us for speaking Spanish; in the history books we were invisible. You learned early on that things weren't fair, and you could do one of two things: You could accept them, or you could change them.

I decided early on that I would change them.

Even though Mexican Americans were the big majority in a number of Texas communities, they were still underrepresented in government. In 1962, the United Farm Workers civil rights groups emerged under César Chávez. For the first time, Mexican Americans were challenging the white political establishment.

The Voter Education Project, based in Atlanta, Georgia, which worked for nonpartisan voter registration among African Americans, was expanding its work into Texas to include Mexicans. I became the state coordinator. Since I could live anywhere, I chose Brownwood, my hometown. I got every Mexican registered to vote that I could and got major employers to hire more Mexicans. We got the city to pave, curb, and gutter every street in the barrio, and to install sewer lines to every household. I wanted to fix things in my hometown, once and for all.

CHAPTER 27

# SHOOTING FOR BIG FISH

*Confronting the racism directed at Vietnamese immigrants in the Gulf Coast fishing town of Seadrift, Texas, wasn't enough for Diane Wilson, 55. Once she got a taste for activism, she took on the polluters who were killing her beloved Lavaca Bay.*

I AM A FOURTH-GENERATION fishwoman. I've been shrimping since I was eight years old. After the Vietnam War, about 100,000 Vietnamese refugees moved to the Gulf Coast of Texas, and suddenly about 100 Vietnamese families showed up in our town. It was tense. Seadrift had four boys who died during the Vietnam War, and another three committed suicide. I was an Army medic during the war myself.

Nobody—not the churches, not the sheriff's department, not Parks & Wildlife—sat down and said, "Let's figure out what the problems might be. Let's talk about how you fish. Let's talk about how a crabber lays out lines—the way we've been doing it for the last 90 years."

Most of the Vietnamese lived by the crab-processing plant; they called it Vietnamese Village. The women worked at the crab plant, and local refugee programs gave the men brand-new boats and motors, brand-new crab traps. When I crabbed, I had 100 crab traps. Overnight, it seemed, every one of the Vietnamese had 500 crab traps. No fisherman in town had the kind of money to buy that.

People's imaginations started running wild. The Texas crabbers used to lay their lines with the traps about 100 feet apart. But the Vietnamese crabbers had never crabbed before, and they put their traps 10 feet apart. That started it. One side didn't speak English and the other side didn't speak Vietnamese. You had some real interesting little incidents. The fights started escalating, but the sheriff's department wouldn't take care of it—it was just too touchy. Nobody would.

The upper echelon of commercial fishing in Texas were the shrimpers. They were higher up than the fishermen and crabbers, especially after the Vietnamese arrived. They pretty much ceded crabbing to the Vietnamese. It was an unspoken vow: You did not dare let a single Vietnamese become a shrimper.

I was running my brother's fish house, the Froggy Shrimp Company, when a Vietnamese woman called and asked me to buy her husband's shrimp. For me, a woman, to be running a fish house was not cool. The men ran the show, and for us to be buying a Vietnamese shrimper's shrimp was going to be holy hell.

My partner—we were the only fish house with two women running it—said, "Absolutely no way are you going to allow that Vietnamese shrimper to come in."

I said, "Why not?"

She said, "They will just take over the bays."

I said, "Well, shrimpers are taking over the bays anyway. What's the difference? Why no Vietnamese?"

We had a knock-down drag-out. I'm usually an easygoing person, but I got so perturbed I took a filing cabinet and pitched it through the window. It stayed out in the yard for weeks. I was resolved to buy that Vietnamese's shrimp. There was no reason not to.

In August 1980, tensions boiled over. A young Vietnamese refugee, fed up with intimidation and harassment, shot and killed an Anglo shrimper named Billy Joe Alpin. In a single night, three Vietnamese boats got torched and a trailer was firebombed. One of the fellows I went to grade school with—so dirt poor he didn't own a vehicle—swam across the channel and set fire to one of the Vietnamese boats. The violence escalated up and down the Texas coast.

It wasn't as simple as some people made it out to be. They wanted to say it was a racist thing. That played into it, but it was a lot more

FISHERWOMAN Diane Wilson of Seadrift, Texas, began by fighting the racism she saw leveled at Vietnamese shrimpers, then faced down the polluters of Lavaca Bay. Says Wilson, "Sometimes you see something and you can't let it lie."

than that. The people who should've been responsible to keep a thing like this from happening were nowhere to be found.

I didn't get politically active until I was 40 years old. I didn't know people. I'd been in this town my whole life and I had never talked with the county commissioner. I didn't know the names of the state's U.S. senators.

Women in the South aren't valued a whole lot. The thing I remember most when I was growing up was hearing people say, "You stupid woman." A woman would go down to the bay and her husband would say, "Get yourself back home. Who do you think you are?"

In 1989 I was doing business with this shrimper who had three different types of cancer. A real young fellow. He had been a navigation pilot in Vietnam and he had these huge lumps, like tennis balls, all over his arm. He brought me this newspaper article, an Associated Press story with a dateline of Calhoun County, where we are. It's a really small county—20,000 residents total—and all we were known for was the Vietnamese problem. But this article said we were also number one in the nation for toxic disposal on land. We were also high on the list in air emissions and transferring of hazardous waste. I was flabbergasted.

Sometimes you see something and you can't let it lie. So for the first time in my life, I called a meeting. I went down to City Hall and told them I wanted to use one of their small rooms. The city secretary said I should either hold the meeting out of town or call it off. The economic-development corporation sponsored by the city called my brother and said, "Get your sister out of this. She's got no business in here." The county commissioner came down to the fish house. The bank president came down to the fish house. One of the plant managers came down to the fish house. The bank president, he said, "Are you forming a little vigilante group here?"

I said, "What's a vigilante?" I couldn't figure out what the deal was. Eventually I found out: The state of Texas had brought to Calhoun County the biggest petrochemical development in 10 years. The deal was worth almost $2 billion. [Former United States Senator] Phil Gramm had guaranteed the permits. His ex-campaign strategist headed the EPA in Dallas, which was going to issue the permits. It was all sewn up. Formosa Plastics was getting $250 million in tax abatements.

I just kept proceeding. Pretty soon, the newspapers started coming out with front-page stories about what I was doing. They didn't want to quote me because that would give me credibility.

It was a sexist thing. They figured somebody must be putting me up to this, because a fishwoman with a high-school education would not be smart enough to do it. Somebody told me they thought I was a spy for the state of Louisiana, and that I'd been hired to derail the Texas project. People said I had an agenda ... that I was a hysterical woman ... that I just wanted the limelight. They even said I must be really profiting from it.

Today, after all these years, people still ask, "What is it you *really* want?" They cannot believe I was doing it only because I honestly cared.

My family would hardly speak to me. My brother fired me from the fish house. My other brother (one of the directors of my environmental group) quit and went to work for Formosa Plastics, which then filed a lawsuit against me. I ended up getting a divorce. My shrimp boat was sabotaged twice before I tried to sink it myself. My dog was shot.

The shrimpers—my cousins, uncles, everybody I'd known forever—

had all lost faith that you could fight, that you could make a difference.

The Vietnamese turned out to be my best demonstrators. Before they go out shrimping, they get on the radio and have Mass. Most of them are Catholics. And usually if there's anything major that needs to be brought up they discuss it on the radio before Mass. I sent out a call for help before Mass, and they all came in like a thunderstorm. They were some of the most energetic demonstrators I ever had. They were ready to kick some butt.

We negotiated a zero-discharge agreement with Formosa Plastics. Thirty-two percent of the water they use is recycled. Two hundred fifty thousand gallons of fresh water are saved daily. Wetlands are being restored. It was going so successfully that Formosa also agreed to zero discharge for air, land, and water.

We started talking about sustainability. We brought the workers in. One of the philosophies quoted in our agreement was, "Do no harm." That applies to the community, the bay, the neighbors, the workers.

Formosa was getting a lot of good press on the sustainability agreement we had. But the issue of the workers was something else. Formosa Plastics has a horrible attitude about unions. By law you have a right to organize, but they brought in union busters.

I was outraged. I had a real disagreement with Jim Blackburn, the lawyer who represented the environmentalists and negotiated the agreement. Blackburn once said, "Well, we should just be grateful we can keep working on the environment." But to me that was a litmus test. The company proved time and again that they would undercut the workers for profit. When you win an agreement, you always wonder if it's just so they can keep you quiet.

After the zero-discharge agreements, nobody was fighting anything. I talked with the workers and learned their wastewater reports were being falsified. I turned it in to the EPA. It turns out there had been a criminal investigation—12 years, over 8,000 pages—and then they dropped it.

I've been trying to get the documents on that investigation through the Freedom of Information Act. I have yet to get them.

At one point my environmental group had so little money I had to cancel the bank account. But, you know, I feel wealthy. People talk about doing things that feed your soul? That bay feeds my soul.

CHAPTER 28

# WHEELS OF PROGRESS

*Michelle Steger's life was transformed permanently when a spinal injury landed her in a wheelchair. But that didn't stop her. Now when St. Louis officials see the brown-haired, 36-year-old Steger rolling toward them with a determined look on her face, they brace themselves for battle.*

I WOKE UP SICK ON TUESDAY, AND by Saturday I was totally paralyzed. I have lupus, and doctors think that's what caused a blood clot to manifest on my spinal cord. They weren't on top of treating it, so the inflammation basically severed my spinal cord. By the time they had treated it, nothing could be done to reverse the damage.

The ironic thing is that I was a special education teacher, and in college I'd been a personal care attendant, so I had worked with people who were quadriplegic. It was familiar territory to me. That's why I think I adjusted so well.

At first I figured I'd still able to get around and do everything for myself. But when I saw the barriers that society kept putting up, it spurred me to do something about it. I was infuriated that I couldn't go out to a restaurant; I had to call ahead and tell them I was in a wheelchair. You basically have to detail what you need everywhere you go. It was frustrating until I learned there were laws and protections out there that people weren't following.

My bosses kept saying, "Oh, you can come back to work." Then, when they found out the injury was permanent and I was in a wheelchair, they changed their tune. Even though the school where I taught was wheelchair accessible, they thought I wouldn't be able to control the kids if they decided to run off or something.

So they fired me.

I could understand that if I'd been a large man or something, but I was a five-foot, 100-pound woman. What difference does it make if I'm in a wheelchair or not? If a big kid wants to attack me, he's going to attack me.

I felt I was treated unjustly, and I needed to do something. I did go back to teaching special education, but I ended up teaching in the city of St. Louis, which is probably the most dangerous school system there is for special education. I was down in the inner city teaching on the third floor of a nonaccessible school, but the kids accepted me. I never had a problem with them. They had to make me a bathroom, because not one bathroom in the whole school was accessible.

They had those old-time freight elevators that a janitor had to winch up and down with a cable, so I could never count on the elevator. It usually took my entire lunch hour just to catch the elevator and get something to eat.

It was not fun, but I enjoyed getting back to work and being able to teach.

I was frustrated that I couldn't go where I was used to going, so I got involved with disability rights and the Independent Living Movement, which emphasizes home care over hospitals or institutions. Through the Independent Living Center here, I found out about ADAPT [a national group promoting community-based services for people with severe disabilities]. Rosa Parks took her stand on a bus in Alabama, and ADAPT started when 19 wheelchair users blocked buses and stopped traffic in a downtown intersection in Denver, Colorado. They said, "We're not moving until you agree to equip some of these buses with wheelchair lifts." They got it done.

We got a group of people together and contacted the national ADAPT office to come out and train us. Part of their training was a direct-action demonstration. We picked an International House of Pancakes that was resisting our efforts to make it accessible. We took our demonstration to the restaurant, where several dozen wheelchair users assembled in protest at the entrance. Ultimately they made a lot of changes.

It's a powerful feeling to be part of a big group where everybody's convictions buoy you up. You know they're not going to turn tail if somebody yells at them or if the police arrive on the scene. Everybody stands strong. That brand of unity drew me to ADAPT and social activism.

When I was in San Francisco, I was flabbergasted that I could get around town. People got out of the way when you got on the bus, and even though the bus drivers had to work hard to pull out these manual ramps, they were gracious about it. Then they would call out our stop.

I can't do that at home. It's not that I want special treatment, but here in St. Louis the bus drivers will blow right by you because they can't be bothered to deal with you. Even people on foot back up into me and wind up sitting in my lap because they don't see me. It's like you're really invisible.

I'm still battling the city of St. Louis because so many historic sites downtown are not wheelchair accessible. Many people with disabities here view direct action as too confrontational, even obnoxious. I stress that we've tried the nice stuff—the letter writing, the polite requests—so when it comes down to it, we're willing to put our lives down and get it done. That's the lesson the Civil Rights Movement taught me.

I try hard to convey my passion to other people with disabilities about how important it is that we be treated as equals. Most people will face some kind of disability in their lives, or they will have a loved one go through it. My biggest challenge is to involve more people and get things changed.

We are surprisingly populous as a minority group. You can't voluntarily join a different race, but anybody can join the disabled at any time. If we could band together to wield that power, we could get whatever we want.

*Stewart Kwoh found his mission in life the year he lost a controversial civil rights case. He now heads the Asian Pacific American Legal Center of Southern California, the country's largest Asian legal rights group.*

Vincent Chin was a 27-year-old Chinese American draftsman in Detroit, Michigan. He was at a nightclub in 1982 celebrating his upcoming wedding when two white autoworkers screamed at him, "It's because of *you* that we're out of work!" The two waited for Chin outside. They chased him down the street, cornered him in a parking lot, and bashed his head in with a baseball bat.

I went to Detroit to meet Vincent Chin's mother. "I want justice for my son," she said. She did not get it: Charged with murder, Vincent's killers pled guilty to manslaughter, and a white judge gave them "home on probation" and a $3,700 fine.

I encouraged Mrs. Chin to try for a federal civil rights prosecution. William Bradford Reynolds, the Assistant Attorney General for Civil Rights, agreed to prosecute, making it the first case involving an Asian American under the 1964 Civil Rights Act.

The trial took place in Detroit, where a black woman judge sentenced the bat wielder to 25 years. After a successful appeal, the case was retried in Cincinnati, where the almost all-white jury couldn't—or didn't want to—understand the autoworkers' racial motivation, which you need in civil rights cases. They said it was a barroom brawl that had gotten out of hand.

Vincent's mother was an immigrant. Her husband, a Chinese American and a longtime U.S. citizen, had died six months before Vincent's murder. She was willing to tour the country to help us pressure the administration; she was a very effective speaker. But after the autoworkers were acquitted, she realized her quest for justice was over. She died last year.

That case was my inspiration. Mrs. Chin lost her only child, and it ruined her life. We need to make sure such things never happen again.

CHAPTER 29

# THREADS IN THE CIVIL RIGHTS QUILT

*Congressman Barney Frank started out as part of a distinct minority—a Jew in Bayonne, New Jersey. Then, at age 13, he realized he was gay (a fact he did not make public until he was in his 40s). Outspoken and decidedly liberal, Frank has been an eyewitness to many of the political struggles that grew with (and out of) the civil rights struggle—including the early Gay Rights Movement.*

THE GAY MOVEMENT WAS CLEARLY inspired by the Civil Rights Movement. Many gay people who had participated in the summer of '64 began to say, "Okay, we're next now." The rhetoric, the arguments have substantial overlap. The fundamental principle is that you're fighting not to be mistreated because of some essential aspect of your personality that should not be anyone's business. That's a common thread for blacks, women, and others. I believe that if the black Civil Rights Movement hadn't happened, gay rights would not have happened either.

Straight white Americans are less homophobic than they think they are, but many are more racist than they care to admit. The Gay Movement started later, but it has gotten ahead. Racism was so ingrained that it could not be escaped, so it had negative socioeconomic effects: poverty, lack of educational traditions, the destabilization of the black community. Gay people were able to escape prejudice by

OUTSPOKEN CONGRESSMAN Barney Frank addresses a hearing in 1998. "If the black Civil Rights Movement hadn't happened," says Frank, a veteran of Freedom Summer 1964 and a strong advocate for gays, "gay rights would not have happened either."

hiding. We paid a higher psychic cost but a lower socioeconomic cost.

The other difference is that every gay person has a large number of straight relatives. Overwhelmingly we have straight parents, and the great majority of our relatives and support systems are straight. Obviously, black people didn't have to worry about coming out as black to their parents; for gay people, it was a lot easier once we started saying who we are.

I think Affirmative Action is very important in the racial context but irrelevant in the sexual-orientation context, because we weren't excluded. Our problem was that we had to hide who we were. So we don't need Affirmative Action, we just need the right to be honest.

Gay people have made enormous progress. They'll never pass a constitutional amendment against gay marriage. Some right-wingers are now saying, "We don't want to give you marriage. You can have civil unions." Five years ago they were frantic about the issue of civil unions, and today it's their fallback position. At this rate, the Gay Movement will be over in 20 years!

Anti-Semitism, too, has waned. Some fringe nuts make life miserable for some people, but there used to be no Jewish Ivy League presidents, no Jewish CEOs. Jewish law firms and hospitals used to be separate from others. Those exclusions don't exist anymore.

One of the advantages Jews have is that they are basically indistinguishable from the majority. The more obviously different you are, the more you suffer the consequences.

Racism has always bothered me enormously. My family was politically liberal. We used to read the old *New York Post* back when it was a real newspaper, when Murray Kempton and Max Lerner and all the liberals were writing for it. I remember reading about Emmett Till, who was 14 when he was killed, my age. He was the black guy from Chicago who may or may not have whistled at a white woman and was murdered. The *Post* made it clear that people knew who'd murdered him, and nobody did anything about it. I was just outraged by that. As I learned about segregation I was really very angry. When *Brown v. Board of Education* came down, I just felt, and still do, that racism has been the single greatest problem in America.

Politics is one of the most integrated businesses in America, so I've been fortunate to spend 35 years working with people who thor-

THE QUESTION of gay marriage remains controversial, but Congressman Barney Frank says straight white Americans are less homophobic than they think they are.

oughly rebut racial prejudice. I've always felt a strong commitment to fight against racism. We're making some progress but not as much as in some other areas.

The Mississippi Freedom Summer did what it had to do: wake the country to a vicious and terrible situation. Had the activists been exclusively black, I'm ashamed to say, the country at large might not have paid attention. It happened accidentally. In 1964, Aaron Henry, a black leader, was running for the Mississippi legislature. Some students at Yale and Stanford, where New York City Democratic Congressman Al Lowenstein had been active, came down to help, and some of them were assaulted. All of a sudden, what had been routine in Mississippi—beating up integration workers—became a national story. That's when people realized the power of the outside focus.

Because of my New Jersey accent, people in Mississippi thought I was not well suited to be a community organizer. A lot of people, white and black, had difficulty understanding me. So that summer I worked mostly as a liaison with people in the North, trying to help organize the Mississippi Freedom Democratic Party.

Living in Jackson taught me what oppression feels like. I knew I was going to escape it in six weeks, but certain people there wanted to do violent things, and the government was on their side—the federal government's response had been shamefully inadequate up 'til then. You had three people [James Chaney, Michael Schwerner, and Andrew Goodman] killed by the cops, so you were totally unprotected. When I left to go to Atlanta, I felt a physical sense of relief that I was out of there.

One night I went down to Vicksburg because of a rumored attack. They wanted a lot of people there. A lot of good we could do! We had pledged to be nonviolent—we were just victims-in-waiting.

Given what racism has done, if you grow up in the city and are walking alone at night in some areas and two or three young, roughly dressed black guys come walking by, you're a little apprehensive. Even Jesse Jackson has said he felt that. But if you were walking at night in Mississippi and you heard voices, you hoped that they were black, not white. If they were blacks, you said, "Oh, thank God." If they were whites, it was, "Let's hide." I've realized there's nothing inherent about racism; it's always contextual.

*When Rev. Kenneth Lyons presided over the funeral of James Byrd, Jr.—the black man dragged to death behind a pickup truck in Jasper, Texas, in 1998—his mission was twofold: He needed to console Byrd's family, and he needed to heal a community.*

Growing up in a segregated town, I didn't understand my role in society until the day my mother took me to the Walgreen Drug Store. Everybody was sitting at the lunch counter. I walked up to the counter and sat down. "You're not supposed to be up there," my momma said. That was my first knowledge that I was living in a segregated society.

Not that it brought any kind of hate or jealousy in my heart. It was just something that was beyond my comprehension.

There was no drawn-out plan of ending segregation in Jasper. There was no blueprint. All of a sudden, the black man said, "I'm tired of this," and he couldn't be stopped. No governor, no president, no army could stop it. It was like an unseen hand said, "This is it, this is enough."

When I was in junior high school, I worked as a caddy at the Jasper Country Club. They had hired a golf pro from Louisiana to manage the club, and he instigated a policy of putting the caddies in a pen. When someone wanted a caddy, they would take a number and that caddy would come out of the pen. To many of us, being in that pen was like being in jail, so we told the golfers we didn't like it; was there something they could do about it?

We had no idea these white men would pay any attention to us, but they did. One day we come up to the country club and the pen is down. The pro, he's gone back to Louisiana.

You're talking about some happy caddies. Jasper had some good people who were concerned enough about some little boys that they got that pen removed. That's why I always had respect for the Christians of Jasper. I'm not saying everyone is perfect. But there are those here who believe in what is right.

I saw that same "Let's do what's right" spirit in 1998. We could not let the death of James Byrd be a black thing. It had to be a citywide thing. The whole city was hurting over what happened. That's the message we wanted to send to the world: It was from both sides of the tracks. There could have been chaos here in Jasper, and it could have spread all over east Texas. But we Christians came out of the closet.

The Byrds wanted to forgive those who killed their son. My role was to encourage them, to hold to the course of nonviolence. That's how I counseled them. Other voices were also speaking to them, but thank God the Byrds maintained their integrity.

We were surprised by the notoriety we received. All those television reporters came to Jasper looking to find a racist city. We didn't want the world to think of Jasper as stupid and backward. We just stood on what we knew.

Some in the ministers' alliance wanted to retaliate. When the New Black Panther Party came to town to march, they suggested we should march too. I said we should stay at home and let them march; that way they won't have an audience. The Panthers kept trying to entice citizens to join in, but they misread the blacks of Jasper. They thought we were angry. They thought we were ready to riot and tear up the city. They didn't know who we were.

Some good has come from this tragedy. People's consciences were touched by this incident, and they made changes in their thinking about equality. The banks and other businesses have hired more blacks, and so has the county. People look at each other in a different light.

A young white boy wore a Confederate flag belt buckle to school right after James Byrd's death. It offended a lot of black people, but they weren't the ones who contested it. Whites came forward and said, "We won't have this, because we're trying to live together peacefully."

CHAPTER 30

# REWRITING THE LIES

*There's history ... and then there's real history. From her earliest years, Native American activist Suzan Shown Harjo has been attempting to set the record straight about her people's heritage. Not everyone wants to listen.*

MY PARENTS TOOK ME OUT OF school when I was in second grade in El Reno, Oklahoma, after a white teacher threw me out a second-story window into a rose bush. He had been arguing with me—or I was arguing with him—about the history of the Battle of the Little Big Horn. My relatives were there and his relatives were not; I knew the history and he did not. He was telling us lies, and I objected to that.

I had already been taught very stridently by my grandparents and parents—by my aunts and uncles and everyone else in our extended families—never to believe anything I read about who we were and how it is with us. They said the white people wrote lies about us. I found that was absolutely true, and that prepared me for a life of not being afraid of anyone.

The only language my father spoke when he went to Euchee Indian boarding school was Muscogee, and the white people who ran the school tried to beat that out of him. I asked him what he used to get beaten with. He said, "1x1s, or 1x2s, or 2x2s," and these are bats, and that's for a nine-year-old boy. That's the common experience of all the people in federal Indian boarding schools: Their languages were beaten out of them. It's ironic that the code talkers used those same Indian languages [which couldn't be decoded] to save the lives of Americans fighting in World War II.

My mother's great-grandfather, Bull Bear, led the Cheyenne resistance in the later 1800s. He was the only man in Cheyenne history to be both a peace chief and the head of the Dog Men Society. The Dog Men Society numbered more than half the Cheyenne Nation at the time, and as many Lakotas, Arapahos, and Kiowas. It's the reason that Gen. Philip Sheridan and Lt. Col. George Armstrong Custer were sent in to raze the Indian world. Sheridan is the one who supposedly said, "The only good Indians I ever saw were dead."

U.S. law permitted generational oppression, and we have had to withstand that. From 1880 to the mid-1930s, for example, civilization regulations outlawed Indian religions, any practices of a "so-called medicine man, heathenish rites and customs, or arts of a conjurer." Civilization regulations prohibited dancing and ponies; you could own pigs, but no ponies. You couldn't travel off the reservation, so you couldn't go to your sacred place unless it was right there. You couldn't have a giveaway or a traditional mourning ceremony.

These were real crimes. People found committing them would be branded hostiles or troublemakers, and these were kill orders for the Army. The federal Indian agent would turn over these Indians to whatever cavalry was nearby. They would go out and pick up the people or kill them if they resisted. That's how Sitting Bull was killed, and that's why the 7th Calvary went after Big Foot.

But my family resisted, and we take great pride in that. I was not socialized to be oppressed.

More than half of all Indian languages and religions were killed off or driven underground during this 50-year stretch. The regulations were withdrawn in the 1930s, but many people still don't know those rules ever existed.

Even nowadays, we have to become outlaws to practice our religions. We go to places where it says "No Trespassing," so we put our lives on the line. We have been shot at many times for moving through someone's territory. In the America I have grown up in, I'm ordered not to do things that I am religiously bound to do. One reason I like writing laws is because I get to change that.

I really grew up in Europe. I was there from the age of 11 to 15 while my father was in the Army, and when I came back, my cousins had stooped shoulders and had been socialized to be oppressed. When white kids would make fun of them, they would just take it; they would put their heads down and not risk being beaten up or worse. White kids used to beat us up all the time. As far as I was concerned, it was better to fight and possibly lose than just walk away; that would have been granting permission to treat us that way.

In Italy I was not surrounded by a constant barrage of negative images. We didn't have people telling us we were no good, or we were lazy, or calling us names. It was very clear that we were Native people and we did things in a different way, but people understood that and didn't disrespect it.

The first time I was involved in a protest as an adult was when Governor Nelson Rockefeller, who had not asked the Onondaga Nation's permission, allowed the state of New York to take land up and down Highway 181 for an acceleration lane. They had started building on the land without asking—the answer would have been no.

The call went out for Native people to come and help.

Even before that, I had appealed to John Lennon to help draw some publicity to the issue. Lennon called us one time when we were on the air, and he and Yoko Ono ended up going to the proposed construction site.

He said, "What's the worst that could happen?"

I said, "Well, you could be killed."

He said, "Oh, okay, just so I know." He was really quite wonderful.

A month after he and Yoko came, we staged another protest just for Native people. The chiefs said we have these treaties of peace and friendship and we don't want to violate them, so we are not going to have arms there—*but they're not gonna build that road.* So we tipped over the bulldozers, and they threatened to send in the state troopers. We waited and waited, but they never came.

Later that afternoon, people started telling us they didn't think the state troopers were going to come at all. They had been diverted to the prison uprising at Attica—isn't that something? The clan mothers at Onondaga said, "We have to pray for them [the Attica prisoners] because they are the sacrifice people for us." That's how they felt, that cosmically that is what happened. In fact, no one ever raised the issue of the highway acceleration lane again. They couldn't afford another onslaught on another race of people right then in New York State.

My role is to amplify our voice, so that more and more people understand what we are trying to do. My first priority is always recovery of land and resources, acre by acre, bucket by bucket. Next comes sacred-lands protection, and there's a variety of ways to do that. One is to give sacred places back to the people. Another is co-management—using historic-preservation and environmental laws, the American Indian Religious Freedom Act, or instruments that protect the places geophysically, because some sites are very delicate and some are overrun by tourists. You have to close them during certain ceremonial periods or divert people.

Bear Butte State Park in South Dakota is an important place to about 60 nations. In the Cheyenne language, we call it *Nowahwus*, or "Holy Mountain." It has springs at the top that feed the medicine plants needed for certain ceremonies. Those springs also feed everything else—hawks, eagles, everyone who goes there. But there is so much development around Bear Butte State Park that the water table has dropped and the springs don't always bubble. Trying to regulate the traffic there, trying to convince people not to use so much water is a constant problem.

This is a place where people go with the sole purpose of praying, yet there was a plan to include a gun range on which about 10,000 rounds would have been fired off daily within earshot of Bear Butte. People go there to vision quest, so you have to have quiet and solitude. People go there to heal, or just to have a final pilgrimage.

South Dakota has since decided to eliminate any and all shooting from Bear Butte Park. We had a good result, but we had to spend an entire year mobilizing. We have to be very creative with our lawsuits. It's like cobbling together a roof when you don't have the materials.

Whenever Indians stand up for any Indian right, it's always as if we are in battle. Well, it's true that people are willing to die for this. But some non-Native Americans talk about us in warlike terms—"Indians are on the warpath"—when all we're trying to do is use orderly processes to perform reverent acts.

CHAPTER 31

# THE LATINO UNDERGROUND RAILROAD

*The torrent of refugees desperate to escape war-torn Central America left John Fife with no choice: He had to help them stay in America, no matter what. The Sanctuary Movement funneled untold thousands of people to safe houses all over the United States—and landed Fife in federal court. In the end, it was America that was on trial.*

I WAS IN SEMINARY DURING THE Civil Rights Movement and the beginning of the anti-war movement. The whole world was being transformed around me. I was able to be at the March on Washington, and I took part in a lot of the civil rights marches and struggles during that time. Those were critical times for me in understanding both the role of the church and the role of faith in transforming society through militant nonviolence. Those of us who were part of that five-year period [1963-1968] and were privileged to march with Dr. King, to hear him speak, to be a part of the folks who were taking some risks together—and who, on occasion, would go to prison together for the civil rights struggle—saw the whole world change in that five-year period.

And that was transforming. It has guided my understanding about the role of the church in the defense of human rights ever since.

I became the pastor of the Southside Presbyterian Church at the end of 1969. In the summer of 1980 a group of Salvadorans was found dead from dehydration out in the desert in Organ Pipe National Forest. That was the first alert that any of us in Southern Arizona had that Salvadoran refugees were crossing this border.

I began to hear about individual Salvadorans who had made it to the barrio and needed food or someplace to stay. We started helping them out on an ad hoc basis. Salvadorans started showing up at the church. I had never been to El Salvador—I knew it was somewhere between Mexico and Panama, that was it. I asked a church official in Washington, "What the hell is going on in El Salvador?" I spent a couple of days back there and they connected me with a guy who was the liaison between the National Council of Churches and Archbishop Romero in San Salvador. I began a series of conversations and correspondence with him.

We had a vigil for justice every Thursday afternoon in front of the Federal Building in Tucson, and began to focus it on the persecution of the Church and the people of El Salvador. I was a part of the Tucson Ecumenical Council, and we developed a strategy to go to the INS detention center at El Centro with volunteers from the churches, fill out political asylum applications for folks, raise funds to bond them out, bring them back to Tucson, and help resettle them here. We're now in summer of '81.

Sometime during that summer or early fall, a fellow named Jim Corbett showed up at a prayer vigil. He said, "I picked up a Salvadoran hitchhiker on my way back from Mexico. He got picked off at a Border Patrol checkpoint. I went to find him the next day because I had just started to hear his story, and he was telling me about death squads and why he left El Salvador. Not only did the Border Patrol give me the runaround as to where he was, but they transferred him to El Centro, California, overnight. And I heard you guys were doing this prayer vigil—and we gotta do something about this."

Jim, who died in 2001, was the most intelligent person I've ever met in all of my ministry and experience. He was always five steps ahead of the rest of us in terms of analysis and understanding. By the fall of '81, Jim is coming to me and saying, "You guys are working on the wrong end of this problem. You're trying to help people who have already been captured by the Border Patrol and they're in the process of being deported. You've got a great strategy for delaying their

MIGRANT WORKERS pick strawberries in a field near Carlsbad, California. Immigrants continue to battle for better working conditions—and a chance to apply their own interpretation of the American dream.

deportation, but eventually they're still going to be sent home on an airplane in handcuffs. When this kind of ethical dilemma has presented itself in the past"—and he pointed to runaway slaves during the Abolitionist movement, and of course Jewish refugees in Europe during the 1930s and 1940s—he said, "the only appropriate ethical act is to help people avoid capture. I've got a small group of Quakers who are going to do that."

And I said, "Jim, I think that's probably a correct analysis, and God bless you, but I'm up to my eyeballs keeping the strategy going at El Centro and other detention centers. Keep me posted about how you're doing."

After a couple months, this is late 1981, I finally went to Jim, and I said, "You're right. Sign me up—tell me what you're doing."

I got a quick course in Border Crossing 101, and started helping Jim's effort. Eventually he and his wife had 20 to 25 Salvadorans staying at their little home here in Tucson, and she was ready to divorce him. She came to me and said, "I can't handle 25 Salvadorans jammed into our house. Can we bring some of them to the church?"

So I talked with the congregation about it, and after a long discussion one evening I said, "We have never asked people for documentation. We're in ministry as a church, around people's needs. We're not going to start asking people whether they are documented or not. We're just going to ask if they have needs that the church could meet."

By now, about 25 folks were doing these border crossings with Corbett. Some of the folks being smuggled over were staying here at the church by that time. It took Border Patrol Intelligence about six months to figure out what we were doing. They sent a message through our attorneys that said basically, "We know what Corbett and Fife are up to. Tell 'em to stop or we'll indict 'em."

We had a meeting in my living room about what to do. We firmly believed we were saving lives with these border crossings, and none of us wanted to go to jail. We decided our only option was to go public with what we were doing.

After a series of meetings at Southside, we took a secret ballot. There were only two negative votes and four abstentions out of the whole congregation of 120. It was probably the high point of my ministry, because it meant this congregation was committed to a faithful witness, even under a threat by the government. We made a public declaration in March 1982, on the second anniversary of Archbishop Romero's assassination. We expected to be indicted.

All over the country, churches were equally dismayed and morally devastated by our government's policies in Central America. Sanctuary became a way in which faith communities across the United States could actively and nonviolently resist what their government was doing in Central America, as well as defend the human rights of refugees and their families.

We were getting calls from all over the country asking, "What's this sanctuary idea, and how do we do it?" We sat down with a map of the United States one night and drew up what became known as the New Underground Railroad to move folks from the border to anywhere in the United States where a church or synagogue had declared sanctuary, or to Canada. That worked amazingly well. We modeled it on the old Underground Railroad, where people knew only who was bringing folks to them and what the next stop was. We never lost anybody.

The significant part about the Sanctuary Movement was that we always tried to base everything in faith communities rather than on individuals. The Latin American model of Christian-based communities sustains itself much better than the North American models, in which you have a whole group of individuals who buy memberships in an organization for social change and get a membership card. Those movements don't endure nearly as well as committed faith-based communities.

I was finally arrested on a Monday morning in January 1985. I was exhausted. At about eight in the morning somebody's pounding on my door. I thought, to hell with it! I'm not answering the door! I *gotta* get some sleep.

The person kept pounding on the door, and I thought something must be wrong at the church. We were living right next door to the church then, and there were usually between 50 and 100 Central Americans sleeping at the church every night. So finally I dragged myself out of bed, pulled on a pair of pants, wandered down the hall, and there's a Border Patrol car in the driveway, a couple of Border

Patrol agents, and somebody from the U.S. Attorney's Office at the front door.

All I could think of was, I got a whole church full of Central Americans over there. I don't know what's going on, but I gotta keep these guys here. So I opened the door, and they said, "We have an indictment to serve."

I said, "Come in!"

I want you guys in here, I was thinking to myself. I figured somebody at the church would see the Border Patrol car and have sense enough to get people out. I put on a pot of coffee and said, "Can I get you guys coffee?" I was stalling. As it happens, the Border Patrol never went near the church.

The trial didn't start until October '85, but we still did border crossings, and we were still providing sanctuary at Southside. We kept the New Underground Railroad operating and formed a National Legal Defense Fund that raised $1.2 million. Stanford University became a sanctuary by a vote of the student body and faculty. Almost the whole University of California system did. City councils in New York, Chicago, Los Angeles, and San Francisco instructed their public employees not to cooperate with immigration officials and became cities of sanctuary.

*Rev. Fife had been indicted for transporting aliens, harboring them, and conspiracy to break federal law. Fifteen others were charged with similar crimes. He and his codefendants put together a legal team of experts in conspiracy law, criminal defense, and human rights. Volunteers came from all over the country; observers arrived from throughout the world. Two days before the jury trial began in October 1985, Federal District Court Judge Earl Carroll ruled that the defendants couldn't talk about refugee law, conditions in Central America, or religious faith.*

It was a long trial, six months, and it was just the government putting on their case. We didn't mount a defense.

Eight of us were convicted and three were found innocent. The first person that Judge Carroll sentenced was a Catholic nun, Sister Darlene; you know, once you take a vow of poverty, chastity, and obedience, nobody has any handles on you! So Judge Carroll said,

"Sister Darlene, I'm going to be lenient in this case. I'm just going to sentence you to five years probation on the condition that you have nothing more to do with this Sanctuary Movement."

Darlene looked at him and said, "Judge, you haven't been paying attention this whole time. If you let me walk out of this courtroom, I'm going to go right back and do sanctuary, so make up your mind what you want to do."

He got red in the face and recessed court and went back to his chambers. He came back about 10 minutes later and said, "All right, five years probation, take it up with your probation officer."

He had to do that for the rest of us as well. We walked out of his courtroom and went right back to doing sanctuary.

CHAPTER 32

# A MORE PERFECT UNION

*Tawanda Murray, a 29-year-old second-generation Jamaican American, watched for years as decent benefits and fair pay eluded her undocumented co-workers at Chicago's United Center sports complex. She went to bat for them, and found herself a leader in the nationwide campaign for immigration reform to help America's nine million "invisible" workers.*

I STARTED WORKING AT THE United Center concession stands in November 1995—wrapping hot dogs and sandwiches, setting up pretzels, and prepping food. About two months later, we were short-staffed on managers, and I became a stand manager. I had to check to make sure all the merchandise had been received. By January, I was a manager. There's probably about 1,000 workers total at the United Center, and about 200 in my department.

Service workers at the center were being ignored by their union, so I got involved with the local. "It's time for our voices to be heard," I told my co-workers. "If we don't stand up now, when the contract comes to an end they'll run us out of negotiating like we're some jumping jelly beans."

So, about 50 co-workers came to the negotiating table with the company. The attorney who handled our negotiations said it was the first time he's seen this many people around a bargaining table at our site. Before it was always done with just a handshake, a kiss, and a smile. The vice president of the United Center learned everybody's first and last name, especially those people abused by management. After that meeting he started to come up to us and talk, to find out what was going on.

Right now I'm representing 556 food service workers at the airport, so I've been fighting with their bosses too. I took my anger and hostility with our management to their workplace, and that's how I'm able to get resolution.

People have depended on me all my life. I'm the backbone for everybody. There were eight of us children in the family, and they picked on me because I was the baby. I had to fight them all. Growing up in a mixed community, going to school with different people, there was a lot of jealousy. If I didn't fight then, I don't think I'd be able to fight now. I had to be able to stand up to my fears.

In my union training, they said they were putting together this Freedom Ride—not just Latinos but African Americans, Nigerians, Puerto Ricans, Chinese, Filipinos. With all those nationalities, it wasn't just one group asking for amnesty or legalization; this was for all people. Still, there was a lot of backlash from African Americans against the Mexicans. One lady there complained, "They're taking our jobs."

"Wait a minute," I said. "Nobody's coming here and taking your job. They're getting the jobs you think you're too good to do. Are those jobs supposed to stay open when people need money?"

I looked at this lady and said, "You are African American and your grandparents went through all this trouble to abolish slavery and have equal rights, and there you go discriminating. How can you let discrimination come out of your mouth when our ancestors fought so hard to make our voices heard? You'd deny somebody else, but what if somebody continued to deny you? How would you feel?"

It got real quiet. They were looking at me like, "Is she crazy?" Then their eyes opened. They didn't realize that when these laws against immigrants are put in place, they target certain people. They targeted blacks first. So if we can get free, why can't others be free?

Coming from a multicultural background, I'm related to everybody's struggle. I have nieces and nephews that are Spanish, I have Polish blood, my aunt's from Korea, my grandparents from Jamaica,

I got people from Canada. Not just African Americans have problems.

Then people on the job were saying, "The Mexicans, 20 of them stay in one house." So what? What Mexicans do is pool their money and buy a building—and they're successful. Now you've got a lot of Mexicans in corporate America. People forget you have to crawl before you walk. You got to work hard to get what you want in life, and that's what these people are doing: They want a part of the American dream. Don't deny them.

The government says to them, "Okay, you're here for so long, so we'll give you residential status. We'll give you a green card to work." But then you have these extra stipulations where the process gets prolonged until it doesn't make any sense. These people come here and work—they pay taxes—why aren't they rewarded for their work? How productive do you think the economy would be without the money they're putting in? These immigrants come over here to build our buildings, and they wind up building the United States' soul.

The Freedom Ride changed my life. Four buses went from Chicago, and on that ride we met people who overcame fears they never thought they would. Black or white, we all share the same struggle. It's a good thing we can come together as one and fight on the same issues. It was amazing how we pulled religious leaders and different unions into a shared mission. Even though I was terrified, I was put here for a purpose: to help others.

In New York City we met farm workers and people who pick cotton for $80 a week. How could you survive in the United States on $80 a week? Eighty dollars a week is not enough to cover light and gas. How are you supposed to feed your children? You can't go to the government for financial assistance because you're in fear that you'll be exposed.

The high point of the ride was getting people to open up. Everybody came from different organizations, but when we got to New York all the cliques broke up. We cried, we argued, but we were always in accord. When we gave our speeches on the Capitol Hill lawn, the politicians heard us. And we're following up to make sure they keep their word. If you're in elected office, you either put up or shut up. Hey! We want an immigration reform act.

*Ron Kirk was elected the first black mayor of Dallas in 1995. Five years earlier, he realized a dream when he wangled his way into a breakfast for Nelson Mandela.*

For my generation, Mandela was an icon. He was our King who had not been assassinated. I desperately wanted to see this man, but everybody I called for tickets said, "No way."

I flew to Washington and called my cousin, who's a lobbyist. He said, "Man, I can't help you. I don't have a ticket."

Mandela was scheduled to address the Congressional Black Caucus, and each member had been given one ticket for themselves and one for a guest. I slept on the couch of a friend, Sarah, who was working with the hospitality group. She kept saying, "Ron, I don't have any magic; I can't help you."

I said, "I don't care. I just have to be in this city. I have to be in the venue. I want to breathe the same air this man is breathing."

Sarah had to be at the event two hours beforehand, so I rode with her.

We get there and I see all these young kids in white shirts and black ties. They're obviously the wait staff. They're being briefed on what to do.

I grew up in Texas. Everybody in my mother's family—my parents were the exception—were waiters and bartenders. As kids, we all worked as busboys and waiters at the Austin Country Club and the Sheraton Crest. Suddenly it hits me: I'm wearing a dark suit and a white shirt and a tie.

I look at Sarah and she says, "Don't even think about it."

I took off my suit coat and hid it under a table. I tucked my tie in my shirt and got in the line of waiters. A guy handed me a tray and I went in and served. And that's how I got in to see Nelson Mandela and hear him speak.

CHAPTER 33

# A LIVING HOPE

*The future of black America lies not in the government but in the hearts and minds of good people—and especially, says the Rev. Eugene Rivers, in the church. As proof, Rivers—head of the National Ten Point Leadership Foundation in Boston—points to his own childhood experience in the wake of the 1963 Birmingham church bombing.*

THERE WAS SOMETHING INFURIating about the fact that girls had been the victims of such violence, that they were murdered in one of the most unspeakably brutal ways one can die. You don't beat up on *girls*.

There was also a genuine sense of the unfairness of it all: Why would you bomb a church? That's over the top.

There was a whole range of questions from fairly tough street kids:

What kind of people bomb churches?

What was this country about?

We marched out of school the next day, a Monday, in protest. That was the first time I had engaged in any kind of political protest, and I began thinking: "What's the Civil Rights Movement all about?"

Those girls were about my age [three were 14 and one was 11]. It sharpened my attention and focused my mind on events taking place in the country. It forced me to scrutinize my relationship as a black person to the larger society. It began a whole process of questioning, because now my sensitivity had been heightened to issues of justice and fairness.

Growing up in northwest Philadelphia in the early 1960s, I joined a gang just in order to survive. In my guts I was not one of them, but I could get beat up every day or I could join the gang. We stole bikes, beat up kids at the community swimming pool, fought on buses, had gang warfare.

Given my familiarity with violence, I very likely would have joined the Black Panthers had it not been for the church. When I was about 16, the Rev. Benjamin Smith rescued me from that Philadelphia gang life. He was an ascetic black minister—a Pentecostal, very strong and charismatic—who committed himself to reaching out to young men in gangs. His message of self-sufficiency and personal responsibility echoed the one being delivered by the Nation of Islam, which had better PR. Malcolm X did brilliant TV, but Rev. Smith was preaching the same thing: "Get yourself together, get off drugs. Respect your woman, stop catting around with girls, be a responsible father. Live clean, save your money." Under Smith's influence, I even persuaded others to leave their gangs and attend church.

When Dr. King was assassinated, my awareness was ratcheted to another level. In Philadelphia, that took a tough turn; now you have the death of the dreamer, the pacifist. I remember when the first reports came across the radio that he had been killed, guys who were Black Nationalists, these cats were shocked. They said, "We knew these people were evil, but we didn't think they'd be stupid enough to kill the dreamer. These people are absolutely insane. You don't kill Martin Luther King! We're not talking about Malcolm X, Elijah Muhammad, or any other black extremists—we're talking a pacifist. You killed *King!*"

They said, "King, who was love. King, 'the beloved community.' King, 'Let justice roll down.' King, 'The lion and the lamb will lie down together.' The best thing you had going for you was King, and now you've done it. We tried to work it out—now we go to war. It's on. It's burn the city down. Let's just have it out. The U.S. deserves what it gets."

IN THE EYES OF THE YOUNG, the future is theirs to shape and to change. "The black community must now reconfigure its relationship with the entire society," says the Rev. Eugene Rivers, a civil rights veteran. "We're using concepts, ideology, and rhetoric that are 40 years old."

It was absolutely astounding. These guys in their late teens and early twenties were seething. I remember riding through West Philadelphia and watching main streets like Lansdowne Avenue go up in flames. I thought the United States was coming apart. It felt like the apocalypse. The level of political alienation generated by King's assassination cannot be overestimated, especially among young males.

That's what legitimized the Black Panther Party. You killed King and you got Black Panther Party leaders Bobby Seale, David Hilliard, Huey Newton waiting in the wings. There was this feeling that nonviolence does not work: "It will get you murdered at a motel. They will blow your brains out. If they killed King, they'll kill us." That was their argument.

The alienation was so strong that some Black Nationalists said, "George Wallace for President. Let's just cut through everything else. With Wallace, we get war. There'll be no liberals, no confusion, no 'make nice.' There will be absolute clarity. We understand where Wallace is." It was literally war. For them, it was "Let's arm."

In the wake of Dr. King's murder, and with the death of Black Panther leaders such as Fred Hampton and Mark Clark, the Panthers remained an attraction for a lot of young men. The Panthers' moral and political argument—that the black community was being terrorized by excessively brutal law enforcement agencies—was correct, but their political answer was self-defeating.

I would have been a Panther, no question. I and others would have picked up the gun. It would've been war.

The thing that saved me in that political period was the black church, which taught me to live to fight another day at a different level in a different way. Black preachers are brilliant readers of human character. They know when you're up and when you're down. That's how you command the loyalty of the flock—because you can read the congregation. You're a master politician. And you've got an instinct for survival that goes back to slavery.

The preachers said to the Panthers, "Boys, you use every wrong strategy for fighting." One preacher said, "Listen, I would have more respect for the boys if they ran a real guerrilla campaign that was smart. But they want to get up here talking trash on prime-time television and tell the man, 'What you gonna do? What you got?' That's not how you fight to win. You're getting yourself killed not because you're courageous but because you're stupid."

The preacher was telling them, "You don't really know who you are fighting. For all the rhetoric and tough talk, these boys will give you war. Ask the Vietnamese. When these boys come to get you, you gonna get done."

I said, "Brothers, we are writing checks with our mouths that our butts can't cash. 'Cause if it goes to *mano a mano*, we're not gonna win. My chief contribution will simply be that I become a casualty."

I told them I reject those politics—I reject the idea that all I've got to show for my efforts is a funeral and clenched fists. There was a preacher who sat down one day with a group of Panthers and told them, "Listen, son, let me tell you something about where black people are for real: All we want is a job, take care of our kids and be left alone, and live where we want. We don't even necessarily want to live with these people. If I've got a safe neighborhood, a decent job with benefits, and can send my kids to college, that's all I want. We don't want freedom as you define it. Black people are gonna go to black churches, barbershops. We're perfectly content to live in middle-class black communities, where we've got people that have our same values."

He said, "Listen, we don't want to be around people who don't want us. Oh, no."

I remember the Black Panther Party getting wasted in all those shootouts. By 1971, with the violently suppressed prison uprising at Attica, it was pretty much over. After the Panthers, we had a run of black electoral politics, with black mayors in major American cities unparalleled in the history of the black community in this country. It's just unbelievable. We got congressional power, municipal power, and lower-level state representatives.

The black community must now reconfigure its relationship with the entire society. We're using concepts, ideology, and rhetoric that are 40 years old. The real power brokers in the black community on a day-to-day basis are not black elected officials, but black churches.

We're now back to the black church simply because that is the only institution we control absolutely. The issue for the black community now is public safety, black-on-black crime, and none of the black elected officials has shown up for that. The black community will not be invested in any economic development if the crime continues at the rates that now exist. Detroit is a ghost town because of the crime issue. Baltimore has got a crime rate that is so bad they have an HBO TV hit series called "The Wire" focusing on black-on-black crime. The failure of the leadership of the civil rights industry to engage the crime issue has ceded that leadership to the black church by default.

I call it an industry now rather than a movement because once we got the Voting Rights Act, the Civil Rights Act, and Affirmative Action, the movement was over. Whites say, "It's a level playing field, and if you don't bust your hump and get in, it's because you didn't do what you're supposed to do."

What resulted in the collapse of the Civil Rights Movement was the failure to recognize that the black middle class and the black upper-middle class would be integrated, but the black underclass would not. No one had answers on what to do with them.

There is no longer any significant popular constituency or political agenda. Black people have as much integration as we're ever going to get. The black middle class can go anywhere we want. The 10 million black people locked in the inner cities, however, will never be integrated into white America.

We can't have integration because any time black people move into a school system in significant numbers, within 10 years that system becomes all black. Any time black people move into a neighborhood and the black population tops nine percent, in five years it's a black community. White folks are always going to run. It's okay. I'm not mad; I ain't going to cry about it.

Our big challenge now is to nurture new leadership, to nourish a new Civil Rights Movement. It's not glamorous—it's hard and tedious work. The end game is to build a movement that is not ego- or personality-centered, but one that is focused on infrastructure, organization, discipline, and leadership. It will be a movement in which black churches and their economic development programs function as informal brokers for the black community.

The black America of 50 years ago is never coming back. We must redefine that concept as a multinational federation of smaller black communities. We are now a much larger, much more complicated global community, one that involves black Cubans, Dominicans, Australians, Nigerians, and Afro-Asians—the progeny of black soldiers. We say to them, "If you take advantage of everything we have produced, you are now a member of our community."

We have to aggregate our power, which is what we failed to do the first time around.

Where this mechanism for political incorporation does come through is in hip-hop, which is fluid and multinational. It's the Fugees, Lauryn Hill, Shabba Ranks, and Fat Joe, the Puerto Rican from the South Bronx. The black establishment may not get it, but the young people do.

HOPE RUNS FREE
in Texas at a federally funded
Head Start program,
one of the most successful
social initiatives
spawned by the 1960s.

*Afterword*

# WHERE DO WE GO FROM HERE?

*By Marian Wright Edelman*

AS THE ESSAYS IN THIS BOOK have shown, those who witnessed the Civil Rights Movement were part of an odyssey—one that changed our lives and ultimately changed America. They also show there is much to celebrate in how far we've come, both collectively and individually.

In 1965, the year the Voting Rights Act was passed, there were an estimated 300 elected black officials in the United States. The Joint Center for Political and Economic Studies recently reported about 9,000 elected black officials—a thirtyfold increase. I became the fourth lawyer in Mississippi to take civil rights cases in 1964 and the first black woman admitted to that state's bar. Today Mississippi has hundreds of black lawyers, and two of my former law clerks have served on the Mississippi Supreme Court.

Though the Civil Rights Movement dismantled the rigid system of racial apartheid, our nation still has a full agenda of unfinished business. It was clear to me in 1964 and 1965 that the struggle to crumble the walls of legal apartheid across the South and to secure the right to vote would leave millions of poor blacks behind unless social and economic underpinnings were put beneath the hard-won political and civil rights. Children must have food to eat, a place to sleep, and health care when they are sick. Parents need a job for dignity and wages sufficient to support their families. Their children need a quality Head Start, sound early-childhood experiences, and education and training to build and sustain strong families, communities, self-sufficiency, and wealth. Black youths and all citizens need a justice system that is fair.

I knew then, as now, that those able to walk through the doors of opportunity opened by the Civil Rights Movement would have to look back and share their talents and resources with those left behind. Many younger Americans have been blessed to walk through those recently opened doors and redeem the promise of the movement. As the civil rights struggle freed not only blacks but whites from the prison of segregation and discrimination, the entire nation benefited. Countless black citizens—and, later, other marginalized groups including women, Hispanics, and people with disabilities—gained the confidence and the courage to challenge the barriers they face. But millions of people of all races still wait outside the mainstream of America without hope of a better future.

The day after Dr. King's assassination on April 4, 1968, the pent-up rage, hurt, and grief of poor black communities exploded in riots across America. As smoke swirled through the air of Washington, D.C., I visited several public schools to urge children not to loot, risk arrest, or otherwise jeopardize their futures. A 12-year-old boy looked me in the eye and said, "Lady, what future? I ain't got no future. I ain't got nothing to lose."

He spoke a truth that I and many others have spent the years since Dr. King's death trying to change. I never dreamed it would be so *hard*. August 28, 2003, marked the 40th anniversary of Dr. King's "I Have a Dream" speech. "Now is the time to open the doors of opportunity to all of God's children," he told 250,000 listeners gathered at the Lincoln Memorial for the March on Washington for Jobs and Freedom.

The young boy I met after Dr. King's death had already given up on Dr. King's dream for his future, like millions of children today. That's why I joined Dr. King's Poor People's Campaign—and began the Children's Defense Fund's parent organization after his death—to help lay the foundation for the next civil rights movement to *truly* leave no child behind. It's time to fling wide the doors of hope and opportunity for all our children, especially the 12 million poor children of all races who have been left behind in our land of plenty.

The Children's Defense Fund seeks to ensure every child a safe and successful passage to adulthood with the help of caring families and communities. Fulfilling this mission is the unfinished legacy of the Civil Rights Movement.

As Coretta Scott King has pointed out, many people today know only the famous "I Have a Dream" part of Dr. King's speech. Too few remember his central metaphor—the "bounced check" that America had written to its black citizens. He said we had come to the nation's capital that day to cash a check America had written nearly 200 years earlier. Dr. King reminded us that when our nation's founders wrote the Declaration of Independence and the Constitution, they created a promissory note guaranteeing all Americans the inalienable rights of life, liberty, and the pursuit of happiness. But America had defaulted on that promise for black Americans and issued a check that had come back marked "insufficient funds."

Dr. King refused to believe "the bank of justice is bankrupt." So do I. America's promised commitment to justice must converge with our great wealth to end poverty and hopelessness for millions of people.

Forty years after Dr. King dreamed of a day when his own children would be judged "not by the color of their skin but by the content of their character," it is intolerable that the gap between rich and poor is widening, and that huge disparities of opportunity persist for black children.

- In 1968, 11 million children were poor. In 2002, 12 million children were poor.
- Three out of 10 black children are poor. Black children are more than twice as likely as white children to live in poverty.
- Overall infant mortality rates have declined, but they have declined faster for white children than for black. Black babies are about two-and-a-half times more likely to die than white babies in the first year.
- Black women are about three times likelier than white women to die as a result of complications from pregnancy or childbirth.
- High-school dropout rates have declined for black and white students, but black students remain almost twice as likely as whites to drop out—the same ratio as in 1963.

- If current trends continue, black males will be five times more likely than white males to be incarcerated. Almost one in every three black males will have spent some time in prison during his life.

*Is* the American dream big enough to include Dr. King's and our dream for our own children and grandchildren? It must be. But we must stand together to do whatever it takes to get America to live up to its promise of justice and equality. Dr. King is not coming back. You and I must build a 21st century civil rights movement for our children.

America is a better nation today because of the Civil Rights Movement, and we owe a debt of gratitude to all those whose sacrifices made that movement a reality. It's time to extend Dr. King's dream—the American dream—to *every* child and family. We have the know-how, the tools, and the resources. We may still have a ways to go, but as the old song says, "We've come too far from where we started from to get tired now." The memories of struggle and hope shared in this book show just how far we have already come on our journey toward building a just nation.

Dr. King said, "Ultimately a great nation is a compassionate nation ... One day we will have to stand before the God of history and we will talk in terms of things we've done."

The God of history is still watching us. How will we answer?